THE ART GALLERY

J. Stanley Davidson

Endorsements

"Every now and then one encounters a book and, based on the impact it makes, thinks, "Every preacher should read this, especially every young preacher." You hold such a book. I so wish *The Art Gallery* had been in print about thirty years ago when I was passing through the season it describes. I'm glad it exists now! In a most creative manner, Stan Davidson probes deeply into the conflicted heart of a young minister and, layer upon layer, peels back the enemy's confusion and deception until the light of truth shines clearly into the mind of the reader. I wholeheartedly commend this work to the heart of every sincere minister of the gospel. You'll soon be recommending it to your friends!"

Scott Graham
General Secretary-Treasurer
United Pentecostal Church International

"My longtime friend has written a book that does a rare thing: provokes us to thought. In a world where most of what we read has the consistency of marshmallows, *The Art Gallery* has fiber. There is a depth of meaning. The journey a young minister makes into full development can only benefit from *The Art Gallery*. An elder contemplating the best approach to impart knowledge and wisdom to the next generation will benefit as well. A significant benefit of the book comes from the thought-provoking and practical exercises at the end of each chapter. Now, there is a rewarding mix."

Carlton Coon
Former Director of North American Missions
United Pentecostal Church International
Pastor of Calvary United Pentecostal Church, Springfield, Missouri

From Ministers Connected to Church on the Rock and the Ministry of J. Stanley Davidson

"In a world that embraces non-absolutes, this book is a stark reminder that we must adhere to the concrete doctrines and principles that were "once delivered." Written in a unique allegorical style, the author encourages us to cling to that which is literal, tested, tried, and true. In addition, I am grateful to call the author my pastor who has proclaimed, preached, and lived out the truths of God's infallible Word since my teen years."

Michael Thomas II
General Youth President
United Pentecostal Church International Youth Ministries
Former Church on the Rock Staff Minister

"Bishop Stan Davidson paints a masterpiece that showcases the value of mentorship. Chad Wittman enters The Art Gallery seeking answers to some of life's most complicated questions. It is there that his questions will be answered. Go on a journey with Chad behind the canvas as he seeks to separate man's abstract philosophies from God's concrete statutes. I strongly recommend this book to anyone who has a ministry calling upon their life!"

J. Bret McGlaun
Church on the Rock Staff Minister

"Bishop Stan Davidson has allowed himself once again to be used to bring wisdom to the ministers of our generation. His words are inspirational cornerstones that will guide all who are finding their way along this path of ministerial growth. His passion for building the Kingdom through mentoring and his unique approach to connecting with those in need of guidance shines brightly through each chapter. This is a must-read for all who are endeavoring to have an impact on the world around them as they continually prepare for that calling."

Mark Kurtz
Pastor, Paris First UPC
Former Church on the Rock Staff Minister

"The Art Gallery is a great reminder in an abstract world of the necessity to be grounded in the resolute and solid foundation of the infallible Word of God. The author paints a perfect picture of the importance of the relationship of the mentor and mentee. Bishop Davidson has passionately poured himself into the development of individuals and the advancement of the kingdom of God. In a world that lacks commitment, I am thankful for those who guard His precious truth and ensure it is passed to the next generation with zeal. His burden and ministry are evident and reflected in His life, and I am thankful for the years he has invested in me as my pastor."

Adam Maddox
Assistant Pastor, Church on the Rock
Alabama UPCI Youth President

Acknowledgments

I consider it a God moment when I was referred to Patricia Bollmann. This book would not be what it is had she not stepped in and accepted the role as editor. "Editor" seems to be an insufficient term, because her work went way beyond improving the grammar and sentence structure. Her ideas brought life to the book. Her expertise brought clarity to the message that burned within me. I cannot give adequate praise for her work. All I can say after this experience is that she is brilliant, and her work is far more than occupational. It is ministry— one to which I am so indebted.

While not listing the many names, I do want to say a special thanks to the mentors and elders who have spoken into my life. You are many, and words spoken to me through the years have helped formulate my life and calling. I hope I have done you justice with this work.

Thank you, Jesus, the Author and Finisher of my faith.

Dedication

To the people who mean the most to me.

My awesome and beautiful wife, Cheryl Wittman Davidson. I honor you by naming my main character Chad Wittman. Ours has been an incredible journey.

To the most awesome daughters in the world. Bethany and husband Bret McGlaun. DeAnna and husband Michael Thomas. I am proud of the Christian ladies you have become and the men you married.

To my grandchildren. May this be an eternal link.

To the awesome members of Church on the Rock in Gadsden, Alabama. You have trained me well. I commend you for loving the ministers that have come from this church. You have taken ownership of this calling and given support to each and every one.

And finally, to the ones for whom this book is written—the more than thirty ministers and wives who have originated from our pastorate at Church on the Rock or have spent some time here on your spiritual journey. I experience great joy when I see the hand of God at work in your lives.

CONTENTS

- *God, the original artist, painted a clear picture of truth, an absolute portrayal of good and evil, right and wrong.*

- *The options were established from the very beginning, represented by the two trees in the Garden of Eden. One must choose between the absolute (concrete) Word of God or abstract human philosophy.*

- *The Tree of Life, the living Word of God, is a concrete foundation of absolute truth upon which one should build his or her life.*

- *The Tree of the Knowledge of Good and Evil depicts the abstract world of human philosophy, an unstable foundation on which to build.*

- *Human philosophy is really not human philosophy at all, but a trick of the serpent hidden in the tree.*

- *An intense war constantly rages between the concrete Word of God and the abstract world of human philosophy.*

- *Each of us must fight the inner battle between the concrete law of God and the abstract world of philosophy.*

Introduction

"Beware lest any man spoil you through philosophy and vain deceit, after the tradition of men, after the rudiments of the world, and not after Christ" (Colossians 1:8).

Through the years I've been involved in the training and development of several young ministers, and I consider it to be a highlight of my ministry calling. As I reflect on my life's journey, these investments are among the most important acts of my life. Some of my greatest joys have come from formal and informal settings that I call "teachable moments." I feel blessed when I see many of these young people developing into anointed and effective ministers.

A few years ago, while teaching a seminar for young ministers at a local church, I felt inspired to write a few parables addressing the disturbing postmodern trends in some Christian circles. These stories took on the form of art expressions, and I began drawing parallels between abstract art and philosophy, two forms that seemed to merge together. These parables make up the chapters in this book.

The parables lay dormant for several years, but I could never seem to dismiss them from my mind. On occasion I would revisit them, and after several revisions I decided to present them in the form of a young minister's search for absolute truth and biblical values.

The end result is an allegory comparing the concrete or absolute principles of God's Word to the abstract ideas of human philosophy. They are object lessons for a young minister on a journey seeking for the deeper things of God.

It has been my experience that each minister must walk this road and make a choice. He must ask himself if he will adhere to the absolute principles defined by God or be swayed by the constantly changing concepts of human intellect. This book highlights principles rather than specific doctrines, although I firmly believe those who follow absolute principles will find absolute doctrine.

I invite you to join me on this journey, ask yourself the all-important question, and ultimately decide. As for me, I prefer the concrete principles of God's Word over the abstract ideas of human intellect. I guess I am "the concrete man in an abstract world," the elder you are about to meet.

Welcome to The Art Gallery, a place of art and philosophical journeys.

Prologue: The Art Gallery

Skyscrapers of stone and steel formed the walls of the concrete jungle as the inner city roared to life. People hustled along the crowded yet lonely sidewalks, living life, or at least existing. One of those people, Chad Wittman, found himself in the loneliest place in the world—in the midst of a crowd where he didn't belong. Yet he paid little attention to his surroundings because his mind was wandering through the maze of questions presented in his Religious Philosophy class.

Still unmarried at the age of twenty-five, Chad had dedicated more than half of his years to spiritual preparation and biblical studies. His early years had been spent in a protected environment under the leadership of his pastor. Then his passion to be effective in ministry had led him to undergrad studies in institutions dedicated to the advancement of biblical principles. After graduation he had decided to enroll at a liberal theological seminary, thinking it would broaden his view. Much of what he had learned thus far had been helpful, but this Religious Philosophy course, in Chad's opinion, did more harm than good, as the professor seemed to focus more on challenging the validity of the Bible rather than exploring its depths.

It all started when Professor Clark asked a leading question: "Is the Bible the absolute Word of God, or simply the inspirational writings of religious leaders?"

Chad quickly responded, "It is the absolute Word of God!" This had been an undisputed issue in his mind since childhood, and it troubled him that a professor of religion would even ask such a question.

But the responses from his fellow students troubled him even more. It seemed they thought of the Bible as just another religious book to be dissected and critiqued, allowing themselves the freedom to accept portions that pleased them and reject the rest.

His friend John Foster addressed Chad: "Then, according to you, it's the professor's question that isn't valid."

Chad responded somewhat heatedly, "Well, you could say it is valid—that is, if the Bible is simply human philosophy. But human philosophy, even if it's inspired, is subject to error and consequent alteration through the process of time. However, I believe that God is the author of the Bible, and He inspired holy men of old to write His thoughts. The Word of God is not the private ideas of the men who wrote, and should not be privately interpreted or altered in any form. And that's not just my opinion; the apostle Peter was inspired to say it."

Chad quickly flipped through the pages of his Bible to II Peter 1:20–21 and read, "Knowing this first, that no prophecy of the scripture is of any private interpretation, for the prophecy came not in old time by the will of man: but holy men of God spake as they were moved by the Holy Ghost."

John interrupted, "But this discussion is about the validity of Scripture, so I think it's inappropriate to use Scripture to validate Scripture!"

Nicole Freeman blurted, "But have you thought about what would happen if we removed the absolute validity of the Bible? How would anything get measured? We call ourselves believers, but without any absolutes how can we know what we believe? And what would be left to build our faith on if the Bible isn't the absolute Word of God?"

John, who certainly leaned toward the secular interpretation, said sarcastically, "I don't think it's that big of an issue. So what if there's no absolute? I think God wants us to have an open mind and think things through on our own."

Chad certainly was thinking things through—and quickly concluded that it was human reasoning that was fallible, not the Word of God. He had thought this Religious Philosophy course would lead the class into a deeper study of the Bible, but instead it was influencing them to question God's Word. He defended Nicole's point: "If there is no absolute, then we are simply wandering through a world of philosophy and ideas, with each person defining his own course and determining his own destiny. If man can develop his own religion, then man can save himself, a concept that is certainly contrary to biblical teaching."

A sharp comment came from somewhere in the rear of the classroom: "Why should we let some ancient writer dictate how we live and believe today?"

It soon became apparent that Chad's views were those of the minority, and he found himself beginning to question the very principles that had started him on his quest to become a minister of the gospel. What if his classmates were right and everything he believed was simply philosophy? What would he have to offer the hurting and lost people of the world around him? He thought, "Surely each generation has people who can see beyond the here and now, beyond materialism and consumerism. They are the people who realize life is more than gratifying the flesh and doing whatever the moment inspires, the ones who are searching for deeper things that feed the inner man."

With these thoughts churning through his mind, Chad hurried along the sidewalk, barely noticing the throng of people pushing and shoving their way to wherever. He longed for some understanding in a world that suddenly seemed topsy-turvy. To him, the questions posed by his classmates seemed new, but he somehow was aware that thousands of minds must have pursued the same path, enamored at the sound of their own voices. To him, people's opinions could get rather shallow at times, while remaining precious in the eyes of the opinionated. After a while, human reasoning begins to sound like an oxymoron that says, "We know so much, yet we know so little."

Chad struggled with the issue: "Does absolute truth exist, or is the world drowning in abstract philosophies, theories, and ideas? If there are no absolutes, as many of my generation assert, then their philosophy is, in itself, a nebulous abstract, a mirage that wavers, vacillates, and changes with a person's own sense of right and wrong. It's like an abstract artist daubing paint on a canvas. Does he know what message he's trying to convey, or does he simply create an amorphous mess that each viewer can interpret for himself?"

Chad's mind was so preoccupied that he failed to realize where he stood. Suddenly becoming aware of his surroundings, he looked up to read a sign above a door that said, "The Art Gallery." The building certainly didn't appear to be anything special; its shabby exterior seemed to identify it as a business well past its prime, a relic from days gone by. Yet he felt something drawing him into the building. He would later describe it as a voice calling to him.

That voice had the cracked, raspy tones of one who has seen many days, who may have preferred to remain silent, knowing the greatest wisdom sometimes lies in silence. Something tugged at Chad to enter, and he somehow knew God was calling him to a greater and higher calling. He had discussed the call of God with other young ministers, but these conversations usually left him troubled. For one thing, had the pulpit become a place where human reasoning thundered louder than the Word of God? Were human opinions dictating church positions more than divine convictions? He was too sincere in his calling to take a chance on going that route.

The voice calling to him from inside the art gallery was irresistible. It sounded like the divine voice that had already spoken into his life. He knocked, the door opened, and he stepped across the threshold. His heart beat faster as he entered into a new dimension that would bring criticism and pain, but also deep peace and abiding joy.

Though the outer shell of the building had seemed rustic and rundown, the interior was an entirely different matter. It was apparent that a loving and gentle hand was keeping everything fresh and presentable. Chad thought the curator of this establishment must be highly capable and efficient.

He was right. The keeper of the gallery kept the place in a constant state of readiness, because he never knew when more seeking sons or daughters would walk through the door. No one was ever forbidden the chance to find the beautiful truths that lived within those ancient walls. The Curator approached Chad, asking, "Young man, may I help you?"

Chad stuttered, "I-I really don't know. I mean, I don't really know why I'm here. Something seemed to draw me inside."

Chad's response brought a twinkle to the old man's eyes. "Did you hear an old cracked voice, perhaps?"

Chad looked at him strangely and asked, "How did you know?"

"If I may be so bold, son, I've heard those words and seen that look before. Have you been doing some soul-searching?"

"I certainly have, but something tells me I'm about to find what I've been searching for."

The Curator nodded and said with a smile, "That's what the Master promised: if you seek, you will find; if you ask, you will receive; if you knock, the door will be opened. You knocked, son, and I opened the door. Not many people come knocking nowadays, so when someone such as yourself enters, it's quite invigorating. Come, let me show you around."

For the next hour or so the old Curator led Chad through the various display rooms, stopping to observe the many artistic expressions. Finally, they came to a door at the back of the exhibit area. The Curator said, "Son, if your heart is really searching, you may enter this room. But I assure you that if you do, your life will be forever changed. If you are ready to leave behind the world's wisdom and pursue the higher calling, then you may enter. But the privilege comes with a warning: you will leave here a marked man. What do you say?"

Chad thought about it, his heart pounding. He had become so weary of the shallow thinking of his generation that he was tempted to enter the room immediately. He really had no other choice. He looked into the eyes of the old man and said, "Whatever is behind that door I want it. I don't care what it costs."

The Curator's smile touched Chad's heart as the old man opened the door and ushered him into the room where few are destined to go. It was a room unlike any found at a progressive seminary or a crowded convention hall. It was small and private, barely large enough for Chad, the Curator, a desk, and a cabinet. Chad looked at the old man curiously. Who was he? Why had he made such a big deal about this room? It lacked the tasteful decor you'd expect to find at an art gallery.

Then his eyes fixed on the back wall. Hanging there was the loveliest painting he had ever seen, encased in an elaborate frame. He peered at it closely and realized it was unsigned. Who had created this glorious masterpiece? His eyes feasted on scenery so beautiful it could only be the Garden of Eden. He felt drawn into the scene, as if a force was pulling him right into the canvas. He was going, going . . . then he felt the strong hand of the Curator upon his shoulder and the feeling vanished. Amazing!

The old man smiled and said, "Kind of pulls you in, doesn't it? Well, son, you may be one of those who gets pulled in. But maybe not just yet." The wise old gentleman then peered into the young minister's eyes, and Chad felt him probing his inward being until he reached his soul. Then the Curator said, "Upon further thought, I think you just may be one of them."

As they stood in the sacred room, the Curator told Chad about another young man who years ago had stood where Chad was now standing. He too had been drawn into the painting. After his initial amazing experience, the young man had returned day after day until he began to enter other paintings in the gallery, unaware that the eyes of the Curator were constantly on him. One day he was a young man searching for truth; in the following days he was making discoveries and experiencing the fruits of his labor; after many more days he was a revered elder; then one day he just disappeared.

Disappointment swept over Chad. Had he come so close only to be turned away?

But the Curator wasn't through. "Don't worry, the story doesn't end there. One day as I entered this sacred room, I noticed something was out of place. Do you see that marble-topped cabinet in the corner?"

Chad nodded.

"In that cabinet I found a book with tattered pages made of some kind of parchment. It turned out to be the account of that elder—quite an amazing account, in fact. The parchment is now sealed, but there is a note. Here, read it."

Dear Curator,

I am leaving you now for the last time. Please guard my words carefully, for they are not written for entertainment. But when you see the searching look in the eyes of another young minister, please unseal this book that he may read the account of my journey. I pray his eyes will be opened to the truths I myself discovered in a parchment given to me when I visited The Art Gallery.

Sincerely, The Elder

The Curator continued, "Son, I see the sincerity in your eyes, so I'm going to present you with a proposition. If you read this book and still want to explore this new world, then I will let you enter."

Chad's eyes filled. "I've never wanted anything more in my life."

The Curator unlocked the old cabinet and took out the dusty parchment. He gave it to Chad and then quietly exited the room. Chad held the precious book in his hands, his heart fluttering with anticipation. He gently opened to the first page and began to read . . .

Chapter 1

Memoirs of the Elder

*T*he Art Gallery is hauntingly silent as I pass from exhibit to exhibit. The artist within me reaches out to each painting, as if seeking to bond with each artist through his unique expression upon the canvas. Each creation is an unveiling of the heart, a child born of its creator. Artistry is not a job; it is simply an expression for which one sometimes receives remuneration. But true artists do not work for money, for to do so would corrupt honest expression. If I put food on my table by means of my talent, so be it, but I should never let consideration of profit influence my creation.

My soul searches the canvases from room to room. I float from painting to painting, drinking in the messages that must be felt, not read. Sometimes I stop and my soul journeys through the canvas into the drawing room, the womb in which this creation was born.

I remember the shock I felt the first time it happened. The pulling, pulling, pulling, then finding myself leaving the world of the masses and drifting into the work of an artist. I see the smile on the creator's face as he views the canvas from different angles, and I see the pleasure in his eyes as he says to his brainchild, "Your message is exactly what I wanted to say."

And I suddenly remembered the word about the greatest Artist: "And God saw that it was good!"

The adage is true: "A picture paints a thousand words." The brush of the painter, the lyrics of the songwriter, the verses of the poet, and the carvings of the sculptor—they all speak volumes. They are artistic expressions declaring human philosophies. The stroke of the brush *and the pen of the author not only reflect current trends, but often create the trends. The philosophy of a generation is reflected in its art.*

The psychedelic posters of the 1960s, the music of the flower children, the paintings of bright skies and bold flowers, and the poetry that decried the establishment portrayed the heart of a lost generation. It was a generation that destroyed all restrictions. They tore down the levee, and the river flooded the countryside until it became a swamp. They began to seek the path of least resistance instead of the productivity that comes from restriction and confinement. No mills were built at the edge of the swamp, for the lack of current rendered the wheels useless, unable to produce the needed energy. There was no current because there were no riverbanks to confine and channel the waters. The most productive generation in American history, post-World War II, had given way to the most unstable generation in American history. Out of this materialized an age of free thought—the age of abstracts in art and philosophy.

All of this floods my mind as I take it all in: each picture speaking a thousand words. For example, I'm standing in front of a painting that looks like someone has dipped a large brush into various cans of paint and splattered the colors all over the canvas. A skeptic might say the artist was depicting a childish tantrum; indeed some parents would punish their children for making such a mess!

Don't get me wrong. I'm not denying that this artist has talent. In fact, I find myself being pulled behind the canvas and into his drawing room, and I can see that he is an artist indeed. Artists are searchers, and their art is born out of their searches. They ask questions, find answers, and then put both questions and answers on canvas. I perceive this particular artist as searching for life's hidden answers. He cannot put his question into words, so how can he paint his answer? His soul screams for expression, but what is there to express? It is terrible to feel a message for the whole world but be unable to express it. He stares at the blank canvas, then takes a heavy brush and slings black paint against the white background. His next expression is in red. Democracy and socialism? Profit and loss? Darkness and light? Perhaps some yellow for cheer, for surely one can find cheer in this confusing postmodern world. But he must add blue for depression, something he often feels. He stands back to evaluate his work.

In The Art Gallery, my ears are attuned to the comments of fellow observers. How many have come into the drawing room with me? How many have seen the consternation upon the face of the master?

One says, "I see a conflict between socialism and capitalism."

Another says, "I see light winning a war with darkness."

Yet another says, "I see layers of anguish in the soul of man."

What about me? I see a man asking questions and finding no answers. Such is the world of the abstract. Abstract art is not defined by the creator; it is defined by the viewer. Someone might say, "That looks like a wheat field on a rainy day." Someone else might say, "No, it is inspirational, like the morning rays of sunshine chasing away the dark of night." Still another might say, "Well, to me it looks like someone is venting about his losses on the stock market." That's why I say abstract art—as well as human philosophy—is what each person interprets it to be. What is right for someone might be wrong for someone else. Widen that concept to the abstract world, and you see that right is relative. In the concrete world, on the other hand, things and thoughts and situations are what they are—and right is always right. All must be judged by the absolutes in God's Word.

I walk into another room. Ah! I see the old familiar strokes of a master, Norman Rockwell. There is very little doubt about what this masterpiece is saying. An elderly lady and a young lad sit at the table with food before them. They are offering a prayer of thanksgiving while some young rogues are sitting across the room, smirking at them. Somehow the lady and the child come forth shining, while not a viewer in the house will come to the defense of the rogues.

Viewing the picture, my soul is drawn into the canvas. I can smell the food and hear the prayer. It is a land where right is right and wrong is wrong—and everyone knows the difference. The parameters are clearly defined. The people in the painting do not know I am there, but I experience their moment frozen in time by the skilled hand of a master. Rockwell's message comes across loud and clear.

Concrete—the message comes from the creator who knows what he wants to say and knows when he has said it correctly. Thus, the concrete message is defined by the author, while the abstract message is defined (interpreted) by the viewer.

God paints things concretely: "And God saw that it was good."

Conversely, Satan is an abstract artist, and his masterpiece is the Tree of the Knowledge of Good and Evil. This monument of human philosophy has warped the minds of men and women throughout history. Satan insists that truth is relative, that one man's truth is not necessarily another man's truth. He does not want humanity to understand that truth is an entity of its own. Mankind does not judge truth; truth judges mankind.

The art that issues from the throne of God is concrete. It is the Tree of Life. The messages sent by the Creator are clear and distinct, for when God opens His mouth, truth is created. Someone may ask, "If some are unfaithful, their unfaithfulness will not nullify God's faithfulness, will it?" Absolutely not! Let God be proven true and every person a liar. "As it is written, 'so that you will be judged in your words, and will prevail when you are judged'" (Romans 3:3–4, NET Bible).

Are you as tired as I am of abstract thinking? Does your heart long for the absolute? Is there a yearning to find a solid foundation, to know that right is right and wrong is wrong? If so, come on this journey with me.

I look again at Rockwell's masterpiece and feel refreshed. I smile as I look into my introspective mirror. I laugh at myself. Alas, I am a concrete man in an abstract world.

৵৹৵

Reading the words of the esteemed elder sent Chad's mind on a journey into his own past. He was only sixteen the first time he sensed a genuine call of God upon his life. It was a special Sunday, one forever branded on his mind. Pastor Hanson's message had so eloquently led him to the altar where he found a private place with God and eagerly offered his life for whatever the Lord desired.

What better way to spend a life than bringing the message of salvation to a lost world? The calling, the purpose, and the message all had a ring of the absolute; he felt no confusion, had no doubts.

After service he approached the pastor and shared his experience. Pastor Hanson replied, "No cause is nobler than dedicating one's life to the work of God. The best way to prepare yourself is by prayer and study; it will make you effective in whatever ministry God wills for you."

With pure motives, Chad opened his heart not only to God, but to his pastor and other mentors the Lord placed in his life. A passion for the Word of God consumed him, and the voices of the spiritual mentors in his life fed this passion even further.

The desire to be effective in ministry had led him to advance his education so that he would be fully qualified for this important calling. He desired to see the lives of others transformed by his labor in leading them to Jesus Christ, and in order to do this he must open his life to training and development.

But somewhere along the path he became troubled with some of the things he was hearing from professors, who seemed to enjoy creating more questions than answers. Instead of a place that shared his convictions, he found himself in an environment where human intellect ruled over divine dictates. This shocking development left him deeply troubled, and he felt as if the innocence of his early faith was being tested in the halls of human philosophy. It was a lonely place, and it led him to the words of the elder.

Chad leafed through the pages of the parchment, reflecting on what he had read. So he was not the first to ask these questions, and he understood that as long as time existed, he would not be the last. He wished he could talk to the elder face to face. He had so many questions he wanted to ask: Why are people so enamored with the abstract? Why do they resist the concrete? Who is man to think he can redefine the work of the Creator?

One thing he was sure of: when an honest man looks into God's beautiful creation, he sees what the Artist intends for him to see. There is no private interpretation. The paintings of this Artist project a concrete message that has a certain sound!

Feeling as though he was about to receive some answers, Chad turned again to the tattered document, ready for his next adventure.

Chapter 2

The Garden of God

Some people look at paintings; other people look into paintings. In a small plain room at the back of The Art Gallery I find a breathtaking depiction of a beautiful garden. My quest for truth draws me into the Artist's masterpiece, and I find myself in the Garden of God, most often called the Garden of Eden. It is unlike anything I have seen before. Even the most exquisite garden in history, the Hanging Gardens of Babylon, one of the seven wonders of the ancient world, pales in comparison to this paradise. I cannot describe it to you; you will have to let your soul take you behind the canvas.

Shh! Someone is coming! I can't describe the manifestation, but somehow I see the Master kneeling on the ground, forming something from the dust of the earth. Ah, His handiwork has taken the shape of a man. No artist has ever invested so much love in his creation as the Master is putting into this masterpiece.

When His creation is complete, the Artist says, "It is very good!"

I feel a rush of supernatural wind as this clay sculpture of a man becomes a living being. He looks around in wonderment, flexing his muscles as if he's just discovering he can move. He doesn't know I'm there, but the Artist knows, for He is aware that many men such as myself will come behind the canvas. Men with questions. Men seeking answers.

That is why the Artist has kept working. He knew that someday I would come.

Although I can't see God clearly, I can hear the incredible love and emotion in His voice as He names the man "Adam." I soon find that He comes quite often into the Garden to commune with Adam. But I am surprised when God changes His evaluation from "very good" to "not good." He has realized it is not good to leave Adam alone, bereft of human companionship.

Then a strange thing happens. The Voice speaks gently to Adam and he is soon in a deep sleep. With the gentle hand of a surgeon, the Voice takes one of his ribs, the one closest to Adam's heart, and forms a woman. Now the man and the woman are with God in the canvas of the Garden.

Everything Adam and Eve need for sustenance is in the Garden of God: the mist that rises every day to water the Garden and the fruit growing on the trees will sustain their strength and health, but they also need "food" for the brilliant minds the Creator has given them. Adam and Eve must have water for their thirsty spirits and food for their hungry souls.

Adam, don't search for food outside of the Garden of God. Be careful not to consume what you find out there, for others are depending on you! Everything you need is abundantly provided in the Garden of God.

I hear the eloquence in His voice when He says, "Adam, I have given you every tree in the Garden for food. You can even feast on the fruit from the Tree of Life. However, there is one tree in the Garden whose fruit is bad for you. Do not eat of it."

Why did the Creator put a forbidden tree in the Garden? Perhaps one who has been behind the canvas can shed some light on the question. Remember that God does not create abstracts; everyone can tell exactly what He is painting. He doesn't leave anything to the interpretation of the beholder. We can accept or reject the message in His art, but we can't modify it. Man was created in the image of God; in addition to knowledge, righteousness and true holiness, God gave him dominion. Why dominion? Adam was a sovereign man, thus all human beings are free moral agents with mastery over their own destiny. However, this dominion would not have been possible in a Garden where there was no power of choice. If mankind cannot choose, he is not sovereign. There is no sovereignty if it cannot be exercised.

The Artist seems to be saying to Adam, "If you love Me, keep My commandments."

The beauty of love is in the exercise of choice—God chose to love man, and man has a choice whether or not to love God. Love is an act of the human will. Human will denotes sovereignty; that is why God planted a forbidden tree in the Garden.

And one day a serpent slithered into the branches of the tree.

Not long after that, Adam and Eve were talking about that tree. Eve said, "The fruit sure looks good. Why don't we try some—just for a little variety?"

Adam warned, "I can see that the fruit looks good, but we already have enough variety. Besides, you know as well as I do that God said if we eat that fruit we will die. So I'm telling you for your own good: don't go near that tree. Don't even touch it!"

Eve objected, "But the serpent told me we wouldn't die. God doesn't want us eating that fruit because He knows our eyes will be opened and we will be like God, knowing good and evil. You don't want to miss out on an experience like that, do you, Adam? C'mon, just try some with me."

Knowledge is not a bad thing. Learning is stimulating and useful and necessary. By knowledge we live and grow. The downside is that the mind of man can be influenced to make wrong decisions. There are three tragic areas in which mankind is vulnerable: the lust of the flesh, the lust of the eyes, and the pride of life.

> *(1) We see in Galatians 5:19–21 that the lust of the flesh is any type of sinful activity that brings pleasure to the body. These can include sexual sins, gossip, physical violence, drug abuse, and more.*
>
> *(2) The lust of the eyes is to look upon things we shouldn't look upon or to lust after something we know we are better off without. Coveting is a prime example.*
>
> *(3) The pride of life is when one lusts after excess greatness or power. It is the sin God hates most. It makes a person want to take credit for something he or she did—or even something God did. It is desiring the praise of others. It is desiring positions of power over others to puff up one's own ego.*

The Tree of Life

The fruit of the Tree of the Knowledge of Good and Evil brings shame and downfall and the confusion of an ever-shifting abstract world of human philosophy. In stark contrast, the fruit of the Tree of Life is pure, sweet, flavorful, genuine, and absolute. People who eat the fruit of the Tree of Life are grounded in truth that will never change, the perfect law of God that is settled in Heaven, and a God who is the same yesterday, today, and forever.

The Tree of Life produces well-defined fruit; each precious morsel is plainly spelled out in God's Word. The Tree of Life is the law of God:

> *The law of the Lord is perfect, converting the soul: the testimony of the Lord is sure, making wise the simple. The statutes of the Lord are right, rejoicing the heart: the commandment of the Lord is pure, enlightening the eyes. The fear of the Lord is clean, enduring for ever: the judgments of the Lord are true and righteous altogether. More to be desired are they than gold, yea, than much fine gold: sweeter also than honey and the honeycomb. Moreover, by them is thy servant warned: and in keeping of them there is great reward. (Psalm 19:7–11)*

The clear world of the absolute

One who chooses the Tree of Life has the right to eat from all the trees of the Garden—all except one. There is an inexhaustible supply of food in the Garden of God. Food for the soul. Food for the mind. A smorgasbord of rich nutrients ready for consumption by the Scripture-hungry disciple of the Lord.

But one taste from the tree of human philosophy will spoil the purity of the law of God. Its fruit will pervert knowledge. It is interesting that the words "live" and "evil" are a palindrome—the same four letters, spelled forward or backward, forming two different words with two different meanings. What they spell depends on the direction one is traveling. Both exist in the Garden of God.

Adam, Eve, please don't eat of the polluted fruit, because it will cause you to die a needless death. Do not choose the worm-infested fruit of the Tree of the Knowledge of Good and Evil over the pure fruit from the Tree of Life! Do not offend the pure Word of God with human philosophy!

So you have a choice between two trees. You can't choose both because the Word of God and human philosophy are incompatible. What fellowship has light with darkness? The carnal mind is hostile toward God because the things of God are spiritually discerned. There is no such thing as biblical humanism. When giving Moses the Law, God said, "If you make me an altar of stone, you must not build it of stones shaped with tools, for if you use your tool on it you have defiled it" (Exodus 20:25, NET Bible). Chiseling, twisting, shaping the Word of God to conform to human philosophy leads a person into a gray area in the abstract world.

The voice of the Creator booms, "Let there be light!" Light conquers darkness. God's Word illuminates mankind's path. The way is strait and clearly marked by signs leading a traveler in the right way.

Human philosophy—the shady world of the abstract

You have the power to choose what will govern your life. You will either live by the pure law of God or you will wander through in the uncertainties of human philosophy.

Man's mind is the highest order of Creation. (The ant thinks the same thing about himself.) However, man's wisdom is always changing. For example, many ancient and medieval cultures believed the stars and planets revolved around a fixed earth. Still others were led to believe the earth was flat. The point is, what we know today as fact may be fable tomorrow. Human philosophy will adjust to the whims of man's thinking.

According to the dictionary, situation ethics is "the doctrine of flexibility in the application of moral laws according to circumstances." In other words, if every man does that which is right in his own eyes, then every man is right. Swing your fist anywhere you desire, for you have liberty. (But your liberty ends where my nose begins.) Right is relative. What is right for me may not be right for you, but neither of us is clearly wrong. Human philosophy looks at the fruit of the Tree of the Knowledge of Good and Evil and the Tree of Life and defines the fruit in its own way. It turns its back on the absolute tree and feasts on the fruit from the abstract tree.

Forever settled in Heaven

The Tree of Life is concrete or absolute. Morality is clearly defined by the Creator in the Ten Commandments. They are not Ten Suggestions. No man or woman can monkey with the words etched in stone. No computer can delete words engraved in granite. No church council can change a precept that is forever settled in Heaven. Paul said, "If anyone wants to be contentious about this, we have no other practice—nor do the churches of God" (I Corinthians 11:16, NIV). Here are a few different versions of the same verse:

(1) "But if one is inclined to be contentious [about this], we have no other practice, nor have the churches of God" (NASB).

(2) "Now if anyone is disposed to be argumentative and contentious about this, we hold to and recognize no other custom [in worship] than this, nor do the churches of God generally" (AMPC).

(3) "If anyone wants to argue about this, I simply say that we have no other custom than this, and neither do God's other churches" (NLT).

Have you tasted the fruit from the Tree of Life? Or have you experimented with the abstract fruit from the Tree of the Knowledge of Good and Evil? Does your soul long for the simplicity of the absolute? Perhaps truth is not as abstract as some would have us believe.

The end of the beginning

Today has been a sad day in the Garden of God, because I heard the Voice again, and it had a painful, lonesome sound to it. It echoed off into the distance: "Adam, where are you?" Oh, that I could run to Him, embrace Him, and console Him! But alas, I am just a visitor from beyond the canvas.

My paradise is gone. I turn my back on the beauty that will soon vanish. I walk, perhaps forever, from the Garden of God, and I stand brokenhearted in The Art Gallery. Alas, I am a concrete man in an abstract world.

◈

The memories of his Religious Philosophy class haunted Chad. Three times a week for the past four weeks, the bickering and chipping away at the things he held so dear were digging painful gouges in his soul. He wondered what possessed people to eat of the fruit of human philosophy. Maybe because it is so easy to impress the shallow minded. Or maybe because it is so easy for people to become intoxicated with their praises of each other. But most likely it is that human nature is so easily drawn to what is forbidden. And that combined with the enticement of Satan often pushes people onto the wrong path.

The classroom interaction with John Foster stood out in his mind. While Chad acknowledged his own inner turmoil, it was obvious that John had been more influenced by the secular concepts presented in class. One Friday afternoon Chad was walking across the parking lot toward his car when John caught up with him. Chad smiled and said, "See you next Monday, John. Maybe we'll have another interesting class."

"Maybe. Maybe not. I will say, it certainly was interesting in there today. These last few weeks I've learned a lot about you I didn't know before. Like, after everything we've discussed in class, how come you're still clinging to such antiquated ideas? You're starting to sound like an old fuddy-duddy, bro. Wake up. Times have changed. It's time you stopped holding to blind faith!"

Chad's smile disappeared. How could he respond in a way that would help his friend? "I guess I didn't know we had two such opposing views, John. But when Professor Clark asks controversial questions, I can't let them pass without saying something. I guess over the years I haven't made my views clear enough to you. I've always seen things this way, even when we were kids together. It's important to have an anchor for the soul—faith in the absolute, unchanging Word of God. You might call it blind faith, but the Bible calls it evidence—the evidence of things not seen."

"But that sounds pretty abstract to me, being that faith is something you can't see."

"The way I see it," said Chad, "it's the people who put their trust in human philosophy who have blind faith. Their faith is in themselves and in their own ideas of what things are and how they should be. They decide for themselves what's right and what's wrong. I just choose to put my faith in a foundation that doesn't waver, a foundation based on the two immutable things mentioned in Hebrews—the promises in the Word of God and in the eternal God who made those promises. That's an unshakeable foundation, which, if taken away, all that's left is human intellect. So although I do understand your logic, John, I can't put more faith in humanity than I do in God."

John frowned. "I guess we'll just have to agree to disagree."

It suddenly seemed obvious to Chad that each person must come to this crossroads—what one could call a "crisis of faith." While the two young men were at different points in this crisis, they were both in the midst of an inner battle.

As Chad headed for The Art Gallery, he was thankful something had pushed him down the lonely sidewalk that led to that sacred place. He had found the way to the Garden of God and heard the Voice. "That is the Voice I've been longing to hear," Chad thought to himself.

In The Art Gallery, he held the elder's parchment in his arms like an embrace. The more he read, the more he cherished the reflections he found there. He opened the manuscript eagerly, wondering what the elder would reveal next.

The Tree of Life

*B*y now, my son, you know I've been to the Garden of God and tasted the fruit of the Tree of Life. It brought me true knowledge, which is the fruit of righteousness or the state of being right with God. Being right with God requires obedience to God's Word. As John said, "The Word was with God and the Word WAS God." The Word can be trusted absolutely. I know, because I was in The Art Gallery and went behind the canvas. My soul took me on a trip I will never forget.

The natural (carnal) mind cannot know the things of the Spirit of God because they are spiritually discerned. Thus, carnal thinking has led to some weird interpretations of the Tree of Life and some wacky opinions about what happened in the Garden of God. For instance, one such doctrine promotes the idea that Eve's encounter with the serpent was not mere disobedience but a sexual encounter, making Cain the son of Eve and the devil.

When people view the world through dark glasses, the world is indeed a dark place. A lust-filled viewer sees a lust-filled serpent and a lust-filled woman. It is a travesty to depict the Garden as a sensual symbol, as if sexual relationships can fulfill its meaning. Carnal thinking is man creating his own god in his own image. It is like describing the flavor of a Honeycrisp apple after eating a bitter persimmon.

As certainly as a priest had to enter the Tabernacle to behold its beauty, so one must enter the Garden to understand its glory. One must go behind the canvas—or else take the word of someone who *has made the journey. I have made that journey. I have walked in the Garden of God. I have tasted the fruit from the Tree of Life.*

A never-changing God vs. an ever-changing world

The abstract world is constantly changing to fit the mores and customs of each new generation. But the concrete world never changes.

> (1) *The Word of God never changes (Psalm 119:89). His truth endures to all generations.*
>
> (2) *God never changes (Malachi 3:6). Isaiah said of Him, "Hast thou not known? hast thou not heard, that the everlasting God, the* LORD, *the Creator of the ends of the earth, fainteth not, neither is weary? there is no searching of his understanding (Isaiah 40:28).*
>
> (3) *Jesus Christ never changes; He is the same yesterday, and today, and forever (Hebrews 13:8). Jesus Christ is God manifest in flesh, the ultimate human expression of the Almighty, the express image of the invisible God. (See Hebrews 1.)*

In The Art Gallery I stand admiring an artist's depiction of God stretching out His hand and touching Adam's hand—fingertip to fingertip. It is a copy of the magnificent work of the artist Michelangelo, who attempted the impossible when he was commissioned to paint the ceiling of the Sistine Chapel in Rome. A weaker, less talented man would never have accepted such an arduous, artistic challenge. Michelangelo had no experience with frescoes. Still, he persisted, and after nearly four years of standing on scaffolds and reaching above his head, the chapel ceiling was adorned with nine scenes from Genesis, including the creation of the world and the creation of Adam, as well as stories of Adam and Eve and Noah.

I follow my soul as it draws me behind the lovely canvas and enter a world that my finite mind is incapable of comprehending. It is a place where few have gone before me.

Did Paul go behind this canvas? As an apostle, he felt inadequate when it came to his credentials and always felt reluctant to boast about himself. But in II Corinthians 12, he related a story about a spiritual encounter. He wrote, "I know a man in Christ who fourteen years ago was caught up to the third heaven. Whether it was in the body or out of the body I do not know—God knows. . . . This man . . . heard inexpressible things, things that man is not permitted to tell" (II Corinthians 12:2, 4, NIV). I believe this was a personal account. I believe Paul made the journey behind the canvas.

Did John the Revelator go behind the canvas? On the Isle of Patmos John must have kept track of the days, for when the Lord's Day dawned, he held his own worship service. The Spirit took him into a place where few have gone. He heard a voice like a trumpet blast telling him to write down the things he saw and heard; he was commanded to open the seal and reveal it to the world. John has been behind this canvas! I know it!

I tremble at the thought of going behind this canvas, but I know I must go, for I am a searcher. I do not go for personal glory; I will not be able to tell you what I see. I go for knowledge. I go for understanding. I go to see what was there when nothing was there. Once I enter the realm behind the canvas, I do not know if I will be allowed to return.

> *Where wast thou when I laid the foundations of the earth? declare, if thou hast **understanding**. Who hath laid the measures thereof, if thou knowest? or who hath stretched the line upon it? Whereupon are the foundations thereof fastened? or who laid the corner stone thereof; when the morning stars sang together, and all the sons of God shouted for joy? (Job 38:4–7, emphasis added)*

My soul takes me through the canvas. My ears hear the morning stars singing together. My soul comprehends the glory of God. And I hear the Artist say, "It is good."

In the beginning was God . . .
In the beginning was the Word . . .
The Word was with God . . .
The Word was God . . .

With God there is no time—no past or future. He is who He is. That's why He told Moses to tell the Israelites, "I AM sent me." Jesus said, "Before Abraham was, I AM," (John 8:58). The Apostolic Study Bible comments on John 8:58:

> *Jesus claimed that He preexisted Abraham as the great "I am" (egō eimi) or self-existent One. Jesus was the same God who had appeared to Moses (Exod. 3:14). The statement correlated with the truth revealed by this Gospel's Prologue (John 1:1– 18): the Creator entered His created order.*

The writer of Hebrews described Jesus as "the same yesterday, and today, and forever" (Hebrews 13:8).

The psalmist wrote, "For ever, O LORD, thy word is settled in heaven. Thy faithfulness is unto all generations: thou hast established the earth, and it abideth. They continue this day according to thine ordinances" (Psalm 119:89–91).The moral law of God is as eternal as God Himself. He will not change His opinions with each generation; He IS—and IS never changes. What offended His moral nature at the dawn of creation still offends His moral nature today. If something was an abomination to Him in biblical times, it is still an abomination. To ascribe a different moral nature to God today would be to defy His immutability. When God has an opinion, it is an eternal opinion.

In the beginning was a holy, moral, and righteous God. That has never changed. Creation brought the clock, the ticking of seconds and the passing of hours. Sin created a vacuum of time extending between two eternities. Time changes all things, but God does not exist in time. He created time, yet He remains timeless.

My journey to the land before time led me back to the Tree of Life. "In the beginning was the Word . . ."

He planted a tree in the Garden of God whose fruit was the pure Law of God. As long as man eats of this fruit, he is permitted to feast on all the other trees in the Garden—with the exception of only one. When a man tastes of the Tree of the Knowledge of Good and Evil, he is expelled from the Garden.

Godly wisdom is needed to discern where privilege ends and limitation begins. God said, "Of every tree you may freely eat, except for the tree in the midst of the Garden." The serpent came to Eve and criticized God for commanding Adam and Eve not to eat of the forbidden fruit. "Has God said that you cannot eat of every tree?" This is one way to discern whose voice you are hearing. The Tree of Life allows feasting on an abundance of delicious fruits. But the taste for those good fruits is ruined when mankind lusts after the tree of human philosophy.

God loves knowledge. We are made in the image of God in knowledge. The natural man craves knowledge of natural things, but the spiritual man desires knowledge of spiritual things. As the sensual desire sensual things, as the drug addict craves a fix, as the alcoholic clings to his bottle, so the child of God is drawn to the Word of God. Those who have been restored to His image can feast on the fruit from the Tree of Life.

I am behind the canvas. Paul has been here. John has been here. It is good for me to be here.

> *Happy is the man that findeth **wisdom**, and the man that getteth **understanding**. For the merchandise of it is better than the merchandise of silver, and the gain thereof than fine gold. She is more precious than rubies: and all the things thou canst desire are not to be compared unto her. Length of days is in her right hand; and in her left hand riches and honour. Her ways are ways of pleasantness, and all her paths are peace. She is a tree of life to them that lay hold upon her: and happy is every one that retaineth her. The LORD by **wisdom** hath founded the earth; by **understanding** hath he established the heavens. By his **knowledge** the depths are broken up, and the clouds drop down the dew. (Proverbs 3:13–20, emphasis added)*

Solomon has been behind the canvas in the Garden of God. "The fruit of the righteous is the tree of life."

> *Hope deferred maketh the heart sick: but when the desire cometh, it is a tree of life. Whoso despiseth the word shall be destroyed: but he that feareth the commandment shall be rewarded. The law of the wise is a fountain of life, to depart from the snares of death. Good **understanding** giveth favour: but the way of transgressors is hard. Every prudent man dealeth with **knowledge**: but a fool layeth open his folly. (Proverbs 13:12–16, emphasis added)*

> *A soft answer turneth away wrath: but grievous words stir up anger. The tongue of the wise useth **knowledge** aright: but the*

*mouth of fools poureth out foolishness. The eyes of the LORD are in every place, beholding the evil and the good. A wholesome tongue is a tree of life: but perverseness therein is a breach in the spirit. A fool despiseth his father's instruction: but he that regardeth reproof is prudent. In the house of the righteous is much treasure: but in the revenues of the wicked is trouble. The lips of the wise disperse **knowledge**: but the heart of the foolish doeth not so. (Proverbs 15:1–7, emphasis added)*

In walking through the Garden of God, I have found that every reference to the Tree of Life involves wisdom, knowledge, and understanding. Thus, those who are attuned to the Spirit and obey His commands may eat of the fruit of the Tree of Life—ingesting wisdom, knowledge, and understanding into their minds and hearts. The fruit tastes the same today as it did in the Garden of God.

Where does privilege end and limitation begin? Do you find comfort in unwavering faith in God's Word, or do you feel limited by His commandments? Do His statutes represent freedom or bondage to you? Do you find your freedom in God's law or do you desire to be free from God's law?

I am once again in The Art Gallery, having returned from my journey to "before time," but how do I tell the world what I have seen? Can a blind man paint a sunset? Can a deaf man describe the sounds of the morning? Can a carnal man appreciate the things of the Spirit of God? I feel cursed with vision in the land of the blind. Is this why Paul spoke of himself in the third person when he reported his journey? "I knew a man . . ." Is this why John was cast upon an island, surrounded by political exiles and criminals of Rome?

Do you really believe I have tasted the fruit from the Tree of Life? Do you, at this very moment, doubt that I have been behind the canvas? Alas, I am a concrete man in an abstract world.

હ્◈ళ

Were these the rantings of a crazy man? Chad didn't think so, because the words were food to his hungry soul.

Still, he could not silence the caution that warned, "To really understand the things of God is to often be misunderstood by man." After all, every man is right in his own eyes, and very few are brave enough to subject their ideas to a higher source. To the pure all things are pure—but one would have to be pure to know that, wouldn't one?

For instance, when Chad went to Professor Clark's office with his concerns, he had felt the bitter sting of rebuke. As tactfully as possible, Chad had expressed what he felt: "I'm sorry for what I'm about to say, Professor Clark, and please don't misunderstand my motive. But the truth is I find it difficult to accept the direction of thought I'm hearing from someone who is supposed to be training and developing ministers. While I am open to study and scriptural exegesis, I can't help but be put off by the open questioning of the Bible's origins and integrity."

Professor Clark responded sharply, "Closedmindedness will get you nowhere in your ministry, young man. My aim is to open the students' minds to opposing ideas so they can learn to evaluate them and determine what they will keep and what they will discard. That's the whole point of higher education: learning to think critically."

"But, sir, I don't consider my mind to be closed. I just don't want to open it so wide that I lose all sensibility. I'm afraid you are tampering with the very foundation of the Christian faith!"

Professor Clark's face reddened. "Perhaps the foundation of the Christian faith needs to be tampered with! And I think it is pure arrogance for a mere student to claim that your message is 'the absolute truth.' In this hour when the whole world is coming to our doorstep, you should be thankful for the positive influences other religious cultures have to offer."

Chad almost wished he had never approached the professor. He began to worry that this confrontation would impact his grades, and ultimately his degree. Still, he persisted. "So, are you insinuating that one's belief in God is relative to his culture? That my personal faith in God is defined by my own culture?"

To that the professor replied, "Perhaps all religions should sit down together and find common ground and a common belief in God. That is much better than the holier than thou attitude you seem to portray!"

Chad couldn't let that ride, even if he was getting in too deep. "If that's true, then God did not create us in His image; we created Him in our own image. I'm not comfortable worshiping something that I myself created." Those words might cost him a great deal from an academic perspective, but silence at this point would cost him his self-respect.

Back in The Art Gallery, Chad thought, "Confrontations like this would place serious roadblocks in some people's search for truth. But I'm not taking any detours. I'm determined to discover everything the elder can teach me. Besides, I trust the elder's words much more than Professor Clark's." He turned to a fresh page in the old parchment.

Chapter 4

The Other Tree

If the Word of God is the way of life, why does the way of death seem right to man? Because he has eaten from the wrong tree.

Perhaps I was a bit too harsh on Eve when relating her story. But the telling of it has brought me to the part of my story I do not like to contemplate—because it comes with pain. Promise me, my young minister friend, that you will not be disappointed in me and close this book before I finish my story. Like Adam and Eve, I've tasted the fruit of the Tree of Life, but I've tasted the fruit from the other tree as well.

Why does each generation insist on proving its own ignorance? Why do we fail to heed the wise words of those gone before? I am not the first to go behind the canvas, and I will not be the last. I am not the first to see great truths and experience great failure, and I will not be the last. While I was behind the canvas, I saw indications that others had been there before me; other silent observers to the tragic scene. Perhaps you too have been there. Perhaps that is why you are still reading this book.

Now that my eyes have been opened, I realize the wisdom King Solomon was trying to impart to me:

> To receive the instruction of wisdom, justice, and judgment, and equity . . . A wise man will hear, and will increase learning; and a man of understanding shall attain unto wise counsels: to understand a proverb, and the interpretation. . . . Get wisdom,

get understanding: forget it not; neither decline from the words of my mouth. (Proverbs 1:3, 5–6; 4:5)

Why did the wise king allow himself to be brought down by many "strange" (alien, adulterous, outlandish) women after he himself had warned others to avoid them? Why did the man after God's own heart look over the balcony to the rooftop next door? Why are the records of so many great men scarred with failures? And last, why did God inspire the writers to expose these glaring failures? Perhaps it is because He knew that all men would eventually taste of the fruit of that other tree.

Paul journeyed behind the canvas into the Garden of God. But this experience came after a life previously dedicated to eating the fruit from the other tree. We know it was a life he never forgot, because he spoke of it several times: "You have heard of my previous way of life in Judaism, how intensely I persecuted the church of God and tried to destroy it" (Galatians 1:13, NIV). (See also Acts 26:9–11; I Timothy 1:13.)

Why does God allow these glaring failures to go on public record? Because all have sinned and come short of the glory of God! You may not have journeyed behind the canvas, but you surely have tasted the forbidden fruit.

It was with a glowing heart that I wrote about the Tree of Life, but it is with a heavy heart that I tell of the other tree, the Tree of the Knowledge of Good and Evil.

I am once again in The Art Gallery, staring at an abstract painting. The artistry is vague and without delineation. Remember I am a concrete man, and I cringe at artistic expressions without boundaries or commitment. I am out of step with a generation that despises commitment. I can go into the drawing room of the abstract and see the mood of the artist, but I cannot enter the canvas and discover the message of his or her art.

I am thankful I can go with confidence into the canvas of the Tree of Life, because the artist painted a distinct picture. And the Artist saw that it was good.

I cannot go confidently into the Tree of the Knowledge of Good and Evil, for the artist does not know what he paints. It is the same with human philosophy; there's no commitment. It does not obligate itself to differentiate right and wrong.

When I entered the painting of the Garden of God, a distinct message awaited me, and I walked with confidence through an identifiable world. Even when I entered the strange painting of the time before Creation, I found something distinct: the immutable moral character of God. I was afraid that I could not return, but I was never afraid of finding nothing there. God is always there.

But how can I enter into something that does not exist? How can I walk where there is no substantive path? How can I believe in something that is not even certain of itself? How can I stand on something that stands for nothing? How can I feast on hollow fruit? Like the prodigal, I was so hungry I would have willingly eaten what the pigs were eating.

A pig has no regard for truth; he's interested only in what he can consume. The Word of God tells us not to cast our pearls before swine; they have no regard for pearls. Chewing them will only hurt their mouths, and then they will turn on you and tear you to pieces. When you take this journey, my son, you will find many of the swine genus who do not appreciate your pearls. You won't find any intellectual rapport with a pig.

I look again at the canvas and decide it is not for me. Yet I find myself going somewhere, not into the canvas, but the Spirit is taking me to a strange place. It is a lonely, dusty road. My companion is a frustrated preacher. He doesn't know I'm there. He doesn't know the Spirit has brought me to his side. I recognize Paul, and realize we are on the road from Athens to Corinth. It is a road of great reflection in Paul's life. This reflection produces an awesome change and personal revelation for this preacher, but at the moment he is undergoing an inner struggle. He is remembering the events of the past few days.

He was full of enthusiasm when he walked on the streets of the famous city of Athens. He had dreams and visions of a great revival. He had an indomitable spirit and a brilliant mind. There was no mountain too high, no road too long, no devil too strong, and no enemy too skilled—there was no open door through which he wouldn't walk. He was looking for that open door, and suddenly he saw it: an altar inscribed with the words "To the Unknown God."

An abstract altar. "Abstract" worships at the altar of the unknown. "Abstract" leaves interpretation to the beholder. "Abstract" is the god of the humanist, and "concrete" is his devil. Beware, preacher, in thinking that the abstract world will welcome your concrete revelation. They are much more comfortable with a god with no name. They worship better at the altar of the unknown than they do at the altar of the known. They enter the canvas of the abstract and rejoice at being nowhere. They don't seek revelation; they seek ambiguity. They applaud the abstract and crucify the concrete!

They resent a person who tries to name their god. They do not worship truth; they bow at the altar of personal interpretation. Their sanctuaries are shrines that honor human reasoning. They seem to say, "Let's cast all our valuables into the fire and worship whatever comes out."

The high and rocky Mars' Hill (Areopagus) is where they come together to hear some new thing. Do not think it is a quest for truth; they don't believe in concrete truth. Their "truth" is abstract—merely for the pleasure of debate. It is most definitely not a fact-finding mission. Please do not muddle their worship by naming their unknown god. God is a figment of their imagination, and they themselves are not fragments of His creation. The young zealous preacher must learn that those who worship at these altars do not want to be disturbed with something as concrete as absolute truth. But the gospel must go forth, even to this world.

How can Paul reach them? What is the common denominator? What will connect the world of truth and the world of philosophy? If they cannot be connected—and they cannot—then what bridge can Paul build for those who are seeking for the concrete world of truth? Perhaps those few would like to know the name of the unknown God.

To them, "unknown" is not a confession of ignorance, unless it is a confession of global ignorance. The man who claims to know this God will be considered the most ignorant of all—cursed with vision in the land of the blind. Perhaps some will believe, for there are honest searchers in the abstract world. But one must be ready for the ridicule of the masses.

The preacher gets a brilliant idea. He will quote one of their poets: "For we are also his offspring." Surely this will impress them.

> Since we are God's offspring, we should not think that the divine being is like gold or silver or stone—an image made by man's design and skill. In the past God overlooked such ignorance, but now he commands all people everywhere to repent. For he has set a day when he will judge the world with

*justice by the man he has appointed. He has given proof of this
to all men by raising him from the dead. (Acts 17:29–31, NIV)*

*How does one explain the resurrection to a carnal mind? How will the
world of logic ever grasp the miraculous? The fruit of one tree is
"logos"; the fruit of the other tree is "logic." Logic thinks he is god,
and he exercises judgment over logos. Logic says, "I don't believe God
meant it that way . . ." Logic rejects the miraculous, for that would
assume a higher power. Logic says, "There is no power higher than
the mind." So face it, Paul. Logic will not believe in the resurrection,
even when you quote their own poet.*

*The trip to Athens did bear a modicum of fruit in that some
believed and some invited him back for another round of logic. But
most of the crowd mocked him as an ignorant fool.*

*He mulled over all of this on the road to Corinth, and came to a
decision, which is reflected in the initial passages of his first letter to
the Corinthian church.*

*(1) "Wisdom of words makes the cross of Christ to be of no
effect."*

(2) "The preaching of the cross is foolishness to the perishing."

(3) "God has made the wisdom of this world foolish."

(4) "God has chosen the foolish things to confound the wise."

*(5) "The natural mind cannot receive the things of the Spirit, for
they are spiritually discerned."*

*(6) "When I came to you I did not use enticing words of human
wisdom." (In other words, "I didn't quote your poets.")*

(7) "I preached the message of Calvary without embellishment."

*(8) "The world by wisdom knew not God." Just plain old "foolish
preaching" is what the believer needs. Your faith must not
stand in the wisdom of man, but in the demonstration of the
power of God.*

*I will never forget our walk together from Athens to Corinth. We had
both been behind the canvas in the Garden of God.*

*I again stare into the abstract painting. I dare not enter it at this time,
for I don't trust what the artist might be portraying. Such is the Tree
of the Knowledge of Good and Evil. There is a serpent in that tree, but*

he conceals himself among the branches and leaves. If you do happen to see him, he doesn't appear as a serpent but as an angel of light. The serpent in the tree has every reason to hate the concrete and love the abstract. He asks, "Hath God said?" and urges, "Focus on yourself, your dominion. If you think you are saved, then you must be saved. Surely there can be no testimony higher than your own intellect! Therefore, you can save yourself."

The serpent wants you out of the Word. How does he get you out? By getting you into the other tree!

I have eaten of the other tree. I won't justify myself by claiming the ignorance and zeal of youth. I thought I knew so much back then, but it was all in the abstract—my own reasoning. There is still much I don't know, but I have discovered that human philosophy is not human philosophy at all; it is the ravings of a rebellious serpent—the serpent in the tree. What I know now is concrete. I have left "that other tree" and turned to the Tree of Life.

My youthful mind was arrogant. Was the world ready for it? Yes. It was another brilliant ripple in an overflowing pond. Another student on top of Mars' Hill. I dedicated myself to reason, and reasoned myself right out of the Word of God.

"Surely God didn't mean . . ."

"That isn't for today; it was for people back then."

"It doesn't make sense that this person is lost."

"I don't believe anyone is going to hell. How could a God of love send anyone to hell?"

"I don't see it that way. What I do see is . . ."

Oh, wretched man that I was!

Thank God I changed trees and became an honest searcher. I am also an honest leader. Someone is following me. Where will I lead them? Is my wisdom infallible? Have I ever been wrong? Am I willing to risk my eternal judgment to my own wisdom? The Tree of the Knowledge of Good and Evil is always adjusting and redefining; the Tree of Life has never changed and never will change. It has never been proven wrong, for it is always right. To which tree should I trust my eternal soul? To which tree should I lead those who are following me?

He looked me in the eye and said, "Pastor, I do not believe I will be lost if I do this thing." It was a "thing" strictly forbidden by the Word of God.

"Have you ever been wrong about anything?" I asked.

"Of course," he responded.

I took the precious leather-bound Book in my hand, the one I have come to love as no other book in the world. I held it up before him and said, "This Book has never been wrong about anything. To which will you trust your eternal soul: your wisdom, which you have admitted is fallible, or the wisdom of this Book that has never been wrong?"

My soul wept as he turned and walked into the abstract painting. He disappeared into nowhere. Will he ever make it back? I don't know, but my soul yearns for him!

"Adam, where are you?"

In I Corinthians 4:3–4, Paul was actually saying, "I am not concerned with your judgment of me. Neither do I have any confidence in my judgment of myself. I trust only in the judgment of Jesus Christ." Will you trust your eternal soul to your own fallible judgment?

The serpent is still in that other tree. In fact, I doubt that very many would ever eat of the tree if the serpent wasn't there. His promises look so attractive to the human intellect, but they are hollow inside.

The last time I heard the Voice in the Garden of God, He was searching for Adam. He is still searching for Adam. He entered the womb of a woman searching for Adam. He walked the streets of Jerusalem and all Judea, tramped along the shores of Galilee, and climbed a rugged tree searching for Adam. A tree is a good place to get a better perspective, and they nailed Him to it. Now perhaps the world can get a better perspective from that tree. His dying words were, "Father, forgive them, for they know not what they do!" Adam, where are you?

Why should anyone have to search for One who is not hiding, One who is searching so diligently for them? For He is not far from any of us at any time.

The beautiful, moist, chocolate cake looked scrumptious with that lovely coat of ice cream melting down its sides. It tasted exactly as I imagined it would—awesome! And the burst of energy was refreshing. Refreshing and short. In just a few moments the exhilaration turned into a heavy, sluggish feeling, and I wanted to lie down somewhere.

Some foods provide momentary pleasure but no lasting nourishment. Such is the fruit from the Tree of the Knowledge of Good and Evil. The momentary rush that comes with the first realization that you are basking in the liberty of your own intellect soon turns into the heaviness that can only be the result of consuming food with no substance. Then you sleep the sleep of death, a "wise" man slumbering in his own wisdom.

Have you also been deceived by the luscious-looking fruit from the other tree? Have you tried to find pleasure in human philosophy? Have you tried to govern your life by the constantly changing mores of a carnal society?

I am back in The Art Gallery, staring at the abstract painting again. Some of my friends that came with me have decided to enter the abstract. My heart yearns for them because they made a journey into nowhere. None of them could give me chapter and verse for why they entered the abstract. They would rather be with a crowd standing for nothing than to be like me. Will they ever return? Can one return from nowhere? Alas, I am a concrete man in an abstract world.

જ⊷⊷ઉ

The anguish of Chad's soul tore through him as he recalled how close to error—to that other tree—he had come. Even though he had, to a degree, defended his faith, he had also spent many hours laughing, bantering, and philosophizing with his religious friends; that is, until conviction gripped him and he began that lonely walk down Destiny Lane. That was the day he first entered The Art Gallery. Now he was convinced this was no laughing matter.

The elder's words pelted his mind: "Abstract worships at the altar of the unknown. Abstract leaves interpretation to the beholder." That had dug deep into his spirit. At some point, human intellect had become the basis of conversation with his friends.

Like the day Dan Wilkins had jokingly said, "Different cultures have different foods and different philosophies. I guess they can have different views of God as well."

Lisa Redding, ever ready to join in the lighthearted banter, replied, "We're not talking about egg foo yung here! We're talking about people's faith in God."

John followed his usual line of thought by saying, "Who are we to force our culture upon other people like the nineteenth-century missionaries used to do to their converts? We have our 'holy men' and they have their 'holy men.' They just do not claim that theirs are holier than everyone else's."

Dan interjected, "But who decides who is holy? Will defining our own 'holy men,' enable us to define our own holiness?"

Nicole Freeman said, "As it was in the days of the judges of Israel, every man is doing what is right in his own eyes. I'm sorry, guys, but I need something more absolute than that!"

John's reply was shocking: "Humanity is absolute. Getting up in the morning and going to class is absolute. Getting a job and providing for your family is absolute. But you guys seem to be looking for the absolute in some 'pie in the sky' dogma. Put your faith in the unknown if you must, but I'm going to place my faith in the known!" John Foster had left the gabfest highly agitated. He now considered himself to be enlightened and his friends stuck in old ideas.

Chad was troubled by the serious questions and ideas coming from John. Where was the friend of his youth, the one who used to join him in prayer and study with a similar zeal and passion? John's quest into the realm of human philosophy was not only tainting his belief in truth, but he was beginning to waver in his basic belief in God!

While each of the friends was going through this battle in his own way, Nicole was the one whose ideas seemed more in line with Chad's. She said with a sense of anguish, "Life was better when faith was simpler. All this reasoning and questioning disturbs my spirit."

What was it the elder had written? "Beware, preacher, in thinking that the abstract world will welcome your concrete revelation. They are much more comfortable with a god with no name. They worship better at the altar of the unknown than they do at the altar of the known. They enter the canvas of the abstract and rejoice at being nowhere. They don't seek revelation; they seek ambiguity. They applaud the abstract and crucify the concrete! They resent a person who tries to name their god. They do not worship truth; they bow at the altar of personal interpretation. Their sanctuaries are shrines that honor human reasoning. They seem to say, 'Let's cast all our valuables into the fire and worship whatever comes out.'"

He had come so close to listening to the voices of human reasoning. His childlike faith had been weighed in the balance, and he now felt condemned over some of the thoughts that had entered his mind. Thank God for that lonely walk that had seemed so random at the time, but now appeared to be divinely guided. He didn't know where his friends were going to end up, but he knew where his own steps were leading him—back to The Art Gallery and the words of the elder.

Chad found himself standing alone, holding the tattered document that contained the cherished words of the elder. The Curator was somewhere else in The Art Gallery, but Chad didn't need to ask him anything. He knew he would find answers to all of his questions in the pages of the old manuscript. And with that, he turned another page.

Chapter 5

A Deeper Look

I stand before a unique painting, the artist's conception of the Tree of the Knowledge of Good and Evil. He has attempted to paint the unpaintable. How can one paint nothing?

But am I not attempting with words the very thing he attempted with brush and canvas? Am I not trying to convey a concrete view of the abstract? Such an endeavor is surely destined to failure. Concrete people will recognize my effort, but abstract people will fail to understand my message. A concrete fact is hard to view with abstract eyes, just as an abstract concept is difficult to examine through concrete eyes. But it's not impossible, for the concrete is capable of exposing the abstract. Yes, the Artist can paint a concrete picture of the Tree of the Knowledge of Good and Evil, but will it be seen by all?

No one can see when their eyes are closed!

My eyes are open as I stand before the canvas. Once again my soul takes me into the Tree of the Knowledge of Good and Evil. I must go one step at a time, for this tree is revealed one layer at a time. The first thing I see is foliage. Beautiful, rich foliage. It is what the world has to offer.

No one can deny there is some beauty here. After all, one can enjoy the pleasures of sin for a season. The way of sin can be alluring; not one man has escaped its appeal. Alas, we must all lose our coat of many colors, our fatherly gift of innocence. And we must all lose our robe of integrity, the one we purchased for ourselves but left in the hands of Potiphar's wife. Our own efforts at righteousness come crashing down, many times accompanied by the sting of false accusation. But if we keep doing the right thing, we will one day be granted a robe by the King. No one can take away the robe of glory! That robe is woven in grace and stained by the blood of the Lamb.

But how can I compare myself to Joseph? My brothers did not sell me into slavery; I sold myself. It was the allure of the beautiful foliage on the tree. How can something look so good and yet be so bad? If misery loves company, then I have had many companions throughout history.

Noah saved the world and then embarrassed himself in a drunken stupor. Abraham was the father of the faithful, yet started a very bad trend in his family by alleging his wife was his sister. Isaac carried it further with an outright lie. Jacob told many lies—five lies in a matter of verses! (See Genesis 27:18–24.) While the family blessing was being passed down, the family curse was also growing. Abraham insinuated a lie. Isaac told a lie. Jacob lived a lie, and until a special meeting with God on the backside of the desert, it seemed that the family curse would defeat the family blessing. Once again, mercy stepped in and a supplanter became a prince.

Samson was mightily used of God, only to be seduced by a heathen woman. King Saul was a spiritual giant, but success drove him into rebellion. David was a man after God's own heart, but he fell to the vicious sword of lust. Solomon spoke words of great wisdom, but lived foolishly.

Before we become too critical of others, though, let us take a true look within. If the fruit of the Tree of the Knowledge of Good and Evil is so bitter, then why have we eaten its fruit? There is a time for honesty, and that time is now.

The Spirit took me to a room in a certain house in Jerusalem. Jesus' actions seemed strange during that solemn occasion when He took a towel and a basin of water and washed the disciples' feet. They were perplexed that their Master would perform the task of a servant. As they partook of the Passover feast, they all wondered what it meant.

Then the Lord began to speak: "One of you will betray me!"

Most men would have looked at one another suspiciously, as if to say, "I always knew there was something fishy about Peter." (Pun intended.)

"What was Jesus thinking when He brought that tax collector on board? Maybe Jesus never trusted Matthew any more than I did. He gave Judas the purse."

"I bet it's John. He always seemed too lovey-dovey for my taste."

Be these men weren't as most men. Jesus' words shocked them, but their honest hearts caused each of them to ask, "Lord, is it I?"

Let's examine this response. When Jesus declared one of them would betray Him, a wave of shock and fear ran through the disciples, yet they did not begin accusing one another. But would each man have responded, "Lord, is it I?" if he were certain of his own commitment? Was this very response not a confession? It seemed each man had harbored doubts. Each one of them must have recognized his potential of betraying the Master.

They had rubbed shoulders with Jesus for more than three years. They had seen the miracles and heard the Master's teaching. Yet they must have struggled within themselves: "If I find the other tree alluring, then why deny my fascination with it?"

I am behind the canvas gazing at the beautiful foliage of the Tree of the Knowledge of Good and Evil. To the uncomprehending eye it is a beautiful sight! To the gullible, the leaves represent freedom. When people see the lushness of the leaves, they begin to think crazy thoughts. The beautiful law of God suddenly becomes a straitjacket of restriction. Holiness becomes legalism, though in the concrete world they are polar opposites. "Of every tree of the Garden you may freely eat" becomes "Has God said you can't eat of every tree?" Privilege becomes bondage. "Is it fair that God has placed this restriction on you?" The rebellious heart restricted by the law of God sees freedom in the leaves of that other tree.

The prodigal yelled, "Father, I'm tired of all these restrictions. I'm tired of the chores. I'm fed up with the responsibilities you've given me. You promised to divide your wealth between my brother and me. I want mine now! I'm going to shake the dust of this crummy place off my feet. I want freedom!"

Such a one must regrettably be turned over to Satan. They won't learn any other way than frolicking through the world on their own, wasting their substance on riotous living. Some must go out before they can truly come in. They cannot appreciate the Tree of Life as long as they are infatuated with that other tree. Remember I said I can't adequately describe Moses' Tabernacle; you have to view its beauty and glory for yourself. Neither can I describe the hog pen; you must experience its muck and mire yourself.

It seems ridiculous to the concrete mind I now possess, but there was a time when sin looked good to me. It looked like the way of freedom.

A scorner seeketh wisdom, and findeth it not: but knowledge is easy unto him that understandeth. Go from the presence of a foolish man, when thou perceivest not in him the lips of knowledge. The wisdom of the prudent is to understand his way: but the folly of fools is deceit. Fools make a mock at sin: but among the righteous there is favour. The heart knoweth his own bitterness; and a stranger doth not intermeddle with his joy. The house of the wicked shall be overthrown: but the tabernacle of the upright shall flourish. There is a way which seemeth right unto a man, but the end thereof are the ways of death. Even in laughter the heart is sorrowful; and the end of that mirth is heaviness. The backslider in heart shall be filled with his own ways: and a good man shall be satisfied from himself. The simple believeth every word: but the prudent man looketh well to his going. A wise man feareth, and departeth from evil: but the fool rageth, and is confident. (Proverbs 14:6–16)

Solomon knew. He had been behind this canvas.

I have discovered the first layer of worldliness. It is the alluring picture of sin that appeals to the flesh. It is the sex, the drugs, the fun, the wild ride, and all that sin has to offer. To my new mind, made righteous by the Spirit of God, it is appalling, but to the rebellious mind it speaks freedom. In the carnal man's mad dash for freedom he runs directly into the arms of bondage.

It is now time to go deeper into the tree.

Once drawn irresistibly to its foliage, one will inevitably partake of its fruit. Let me attempt to describe the taste. It has a very sweet flavor that provides a momentary rush. But that sweet flavor soon turns bitter, and that quick burst of pleasure soon becomes depression. The fruit of the Tree of the Knowledge of Good and Evil is seasonal; the pleasures of sin only last for a season. In contrast, the Tree of Life bears fruit year round, and the pleasure lasts forever!

Take a piece of deceptive fruit to the laboratory and examine it. You will find it contains three elements. At this point, the abstract world can be defined in concrete terms. Some would accuse me of oversimplifying things, but the Word of God backs up my statement by naming in concrete terms the three elements that are in the deceptive fruit:

(1) The lust of the flesh
(2) The lust of the eyes
(3) The pride of life

The serpent wants you to think he is offering a smorgasbord of excitement and thrills, but he serves only three courses. That's it. And please notice all of those courses focus on you.

There is one sure road to depression and that is self-focus. Human philosophy says, "Look for the answer within you!" But I know the answer is not within you!

A thief walked into a bank with his gun drawn. He forced the customers to lie on the floor, then demanded that his bags be filled with cash. He waved his pistol to intimidate the bank employees, and they gave him what he wanted because their lives were more valuable than money or possessions.

The thief laughed and darted out the door, only to encounter something he hadn't planned on: a police officer passing by on his way home from work. The officer quickly assessed the situation, drew his gun, and shouted, "Stop!"

The thief whirled around to run but thought better of it and aimed his pistol at the policemen. It was his last act on earth. The thief coughed out his life's blood as he lay across the bags of money.

He found himself in another world, following a white-robed being who refused to answer any of his questions. He had an inkling of what to expect, though, for he remembered his mother warning him about the life of degradation he was leading. He recalled some sermons from the few times he had sat on a church pew. If those sermons were correct, he was in for a horrible future. Trepidation filled him as he followed the white-robed being down a long hallway.

They stopped before a door, and the thief braced himself for what he would find on the other side of the door. You can't imagine the shock of what he found.

Beautiful women were everywhere! He looked at his guide in disbelief, but the insinuation was obvious. They were his women! What kind of world had he come to? His narrow mind defined it as

Heaven, but how had he managed to come to Heaven? He had always loved the pool halls, the smoke-filled air, the gambling, the cards, and the dim lights. He was pleased to see a pool table with the balls already racked for him. He chose a cue stick and broke. Amazing! All the balls went into the pockets. He did this once more. Then three, six, ten, twenty times! What boredom! He decided to go on to something else.

How about a game of cards? He drew four cards from the deck. Four aces! He drew again. Four aces. One time. Ten times. Thirty times. This was crazy!

Everything he touched became what he wanted it to be. He would feel an initial rush of excitement but would quickly get bored. Then irritated. Then maddened. He began to hate the beautiful women. He began to hate the pool table and the deck of cards. He became a raving maniac.

He ran to the white-robed guide, screaming, "I may as well have gone to hell!"

His guide opened his mouth for first time and said, "This is hell!"

I read the above story so long ago that I've forgotten the source. Perhaps it is not theologically sound, but it is thought-provoking. Such is the fruit from the other tree. It makes one very hungry, but never satisfies! Some call it Heaven, but I know it is hell. Is hell nothing more than lust that is never gratified? Is this the burning where the fire is not quenched? Is this what I am seeing behind the canvas?

- *Noah's drunkenness (the lust of the flesh)*
- *Abraham's lie (the pride of life) "Why trust in God when I can use my own cunning to protect what is mine?"*
- *Samson's fall (the lust of the flesh)*
- *Saul's sin (the pride of life) "Why do I need to wait on the man of God? I have edited and improved God's commandments."*
- *David's failure (the lust of the flesh and the lust of the eyes)*
- *Solomon's downfall (the lust of the flesh)*

The fruit of the other tree is unique in that it can change its outward appearance to appeal to each individual. That's the abstract part. The concrete part is that it's always the same fruit. It has always been the same. It will always be the same.

Eve looked at the tree. It's fruit certainly appeared delectable. She saw that it was good for food—the lust of the flesh. She saw that it was pleasant to the eyes—the lust of the eyes. She saw that it was a tree to be desired to make one wise—the pride of life. This fruit always tells the same lie. It is a concrete fact in the abstract world.

I once watched a picky eater—the kind of eater that grates on my nerves. He pulled apart a sandwich and inspected the filling. Then, with a finger, he scooped up the tuna salad bite by bite. Then he crammed the bread into his mouth. It was disgusting. Picky eaters are never satisfied with anything. They don't trust the sandwich-maker, so they look around to see if they're being observed, then pull the sandwich apart.

Do you do that? Do you search inside the bread to see what you're eating? Perhaps it's rude. Then again, perhaps it's smart!

You see, one has to beware of "lie sandwiches." They are easy to make. Simply take two truths and slide a lie between them. Religious chefs have been doing this for years. Most people will take a quick look at the two visible truths and consume it, lie and all.

"Your eyes will be opened." True. "You will know good and evil." True, in a perverted sort of way. However, slipped between those two truths is the lie "You will become as gods." That is the mystery of iniquity! Two trees, two mysteries, but that is another painting in The Art Gallery we will save for later.

I'm behind the canvas in the Tree of the Knowledge of Good and Evil. We are entering the tree one layer at a time. The first layer was the foliage, which is all that is in the world, the surface lures and enticements. The second layer is the fruit. No matter how it appears, it is always the lust of the flesh, the lust of the eyes, or the pride of life. We must go deeper to receive a greater revelation. Beware, for there is an element of danger where we are going.

My suspicion is aroused. Righteous indignation comes over me and I begin to strip the foliage and fruit from the tree. In a frenzy, I sling it in every direction. I am obsessed with the need to expose this lie once and for all. I am angry at being deceived. I am angry that those I love have been deceived. I want to strip this lying tree bare and expose the deceiver.

The lie is that there's no such thing as "human philosophy." It is all a façade. The carnal man is a mere puppet in the hands of the puppeteer. The puppeteer allows man to take credit for his ideas, but they are not man's ideas at all! When he questions the Word of God, he is not thinking his own thoughts; he is echoing the thoughts of the master rebel! Human philosophy is a masquerade!

Face the brutal reality, my friend. The Tree of Life is the law of God. The Tree of the Knowledge of Good and Evil is the law of Satan. Mankind has no law of his own. His law (flesh) is a borrowed law. Mankind simply chooses between the two existing laws.

Get past the foliage. Get past the fruit. The tree has been stripped bare by this mad concrete artist to expose the third layer: a poisonous serpent in the tree!

It is the third dimension of worldliness—the pride of life.

That is why philosophy is abstract: the serpent cannot exist in an arena of truth. Disguise is his insurance. Deceit is his camouflage. The world of the abstract is his heaven. The concrete absolute is his hell. Lies bind people. Truth sets people free.

You can wander in your vague world of flashy foliage and fancy fruit, but your abstract mirage is just a covering for an old evil. Take "evil" and add a "d." You will find your abstract mirage is just a covering for an old devil!

There is a serpent in the tree. Anytime you see the leaves of worldliness and the fruit of compromise, be assured that there is a serpent in the tree.

Are you still fascinated by this tree? Sin fascinates, then assassinates! Have you seen the truth? Does the façade of sin anger you? If so, read on, for we are on the same journey.

My fit of rage subsides. It is just a painting after all. I turn and slowly but angrily walk back through the canvas into The Art Gallery. The picture is now clear to me. There is no such thing as human philosophy. I am the sinner after the sin has taken place. My pleasure is now guilt. My laughter is now sorrow.

But I did return, and I have learned my lesson. I now eat from the Tree of Life. I am now a concrete man in an abstract world.

❧◦❦

The group of friends were gathered at the Campus Café, one of their favorite meeting places for after-class confab sessions. Over sandwiches, salads, and shakes, Dan Wilkins jokingly asked, "Where's Brother Head-in-the-clouds today? Locked away in his holy closet again? He used to be more fun to be around!"

John Foster said, "I've known him longer than any of you, and I remember we had a lot of fun times when we were young. But lately he's got a bee in his bonnet—getting too spiritual for me. He's probably off somewhere polishing his halo. Maybe we should follow him sometime to see where he goes."

Dan, ever the one searching for the path of least resistance, commented, "Wherever he is, I think he's getting in a little too deep. All he wants to do is lock himself in his room and study. He seems to have lost the ability to enjoy life."

Lisa Redding reflected, "Well, I grant you he's been pretty serious lately, but I miss him, and some of the questions he's been asking are good ones."

Dan was quick to retort, "Well, our lives will be serious enough once we graduate. I'm more into having a good time while I can. Sometimes I get tired of having to be on what Chad calls a spiritual vigil."

John added his usual sarcasm. "Well, he can question everything and cram his head full of religious conundrums if he wants, but I believe God created life to be enjoyed. Some people are too heavenly minded to be of any earthly good. In spite of what Chad says, I think Professor Clark has been making some very interesting points. In fact, some of it seems quite liberating to me!"

Nicole once again inserted a voice of caution. "But aren't more problems caused by those who are too earthly minded to be of any heavenly good? Aren't they falling for the same trick that led Eve to eat of the fruit? What a person's mind and flesh define as pleasure and what his soul and spirit define as pleasure are usually not the same things. I prefer to find my greatest pleasure in the things of God."

"Now don't you get all holy on us," John blurted. "You're starting to sound like Chad, or worse, the ten thousand lectures my parents gave me growing up. After all, who made up the so-called code of ethics? I think it's every man for himself. As Professor Clark suggested, each individual knows what's right or wrong in their own context. And I think ministers who help people feel good about themselves are making the world a better place. People don't need or want to be harassed by prophets of doom."

Nicole frowned. "I read in Genesis about man's thoughts being only evil continually. I concede every person has the inward potential for good, but the psalmist said man's heart is deceitful. I don't think God allows for everyone to create their own set of rules, else why would He have sent the Flood? I feel a lot safer letting the Word of God guide me."

Lisa said, "That's all well and good, but getting back to Chad, I'm still wondering what's so important that he doesn't have time for his friends anymore. Where is he anyway?"

John said, "I was teasing when I suggested we follow him. I already know where he goes—to that old Art Gallery. Every day. Right after class."

Dan asked incredulously, "You mean that useless rundown place on Destiny Lane? Why would he possibly want to spend time there? One walk-through would be enough for me."

Ironically, as this conversation was taking place, Chad was thinking along similar lines: "The pull of this Art Gallery isn't strong enough to draw very many people in here. And it can get kind of lonely in these near-empty, echoing rooms. But when I linger here in expectation of finding answers, I also get a taste of reality as fresh as the beauty of an unspoiled morning. In this art gallery I'm finding truth unveiled in all its glory. I'm thankful for the artwork hanging on these walls—even the abstract—for truth is revealed behind each canvas."

He looked down at the book in his hands. Both the wavering script and the yellowed pages indicated the advanced age of the elder. "And I'm thankful the Curator helped me find this precious parchment." He turned the page to look at the title of the next chapter: "The Philosophical War." "Oh good," he thought. "Maybe the elder will reveal some specifics regarding the things we've been discussing in class."

Chapter 6

The Philosophical War

*A*rt is an expression of the codes by which societies exist. *Artists are searchers, but what they find depends on where they conduct their search. For instance, the kingdom of Heaven is like a treasure hidden in a field. Not just any field, mind you. The artist must dig in the right field to find the kingdom of Heaven.*

The choice of where to search is either an abstract field or a concrete field. The expression, the work of art, is either defined clearly by its creator or interpreted vaguely by the beholder.

How can an artist express something that is not a part of himself? To a certain degree we all are artists. Each person expresses himself in some way. This expression is revealing, for it is the fruit one bears. The Bible says we are known by our fruit.

Are you part of the abstract world that is constantly changing its mores and customs? Do you worship at the altar of the unknown? Do you revel in human philosophy? This is a question you need not give an answer, for the answer lies for all to see. And it all begins with one seed.

The curious painting of the dissected seed

A certain painting catches my attention, and I obtain a copy of it for my archives. It is a strange thing for an artist to paint; it depicts a dissected seed open and exposed to the observer. Inside the seed is the power of reproduction. What mysteries are contained in this painting?

To find the answer, I go behind the canvas, and my soul takes me into the dissected seed. Such an innocent, dormant thing, but what a surprise awaits me. I can feel the power—untapped power—awaiting its moment of release, waiting to burst forth in vibrant expression. If not now, then someday it will express itself, like seeds that have lain dormant for hundreds of years, and then, when the conditions are right, will germinate and burst forth—first into a small plant, and then into a bush adorned with colorful leaves. Then, finally, it brings forth fruit.

A layman probably can't identify the nature of this particular seed, so the artist is safe for now. He will not be exposed at this stage. Even when the leaves begin to bud, he remains safe, for the average person is not an expert at identifying a tree by its leaves. However, most people can distinguish between the kinds of fruit when they see it. It is the fruit that announces to the world the nature of the seed. It is the fruit that exposes the artist.

The same tree cannot bring forth both good and evil fruit. The same tree will not produce both apples and oranges. The Tree of Life brings forth all manner of fruit, but is really one fruit with many attributes—the pure truth of God's Word.

My journey into the seed reveals to me the nature of this plant. I can see what it will be when it germinates and springs forth into life. Then the fruit will announce to the world what is inside the heart of this artist. My brief journey is over, and I return from behind the canvas.

The answer I sought comes with a question to ponder: when the fruit finally hangs from the limbs of my tree, what will the world discover about the seed in my heart?

The philosophical war: the well-defined vs. the indistinct

Since the dawn of time, a war has been waging between two trees as they fight for the mind of man. The mind is the battlefield of the soul, the place where the war is won or lost.

"This I say therefore, and testify in the Lord, that ye henceforth walk not as other Gentiles walk, in the vanity of their mind" (Ephesians 4:17). Human philosophy is vain (useless, producing no results).

"And be renewed in the spirit of your mind" (Ephesians 4:23). Our mind must be renewed, or made new again. It must be restored to its original state, in harmony with God and His Word.

"And you, that were sometime alienated and enemies in your mind by wicked works, yet now hath he reconciled" (Colossians 1:21). Our minds were alienated but now they have been reconciled—reunited, put to rights, joined to God.

"And be not conformed to this world: but be ye transformed by the renewing of your mind, that ye may prove what is that good, and acceptable, and perfect, will of God" (Romans 12:2). A transformation, a metamorphosis, must take place.

"Jesus said unto him, Thou shalt love the Lord thy God with all thy heart, and with all thy soul, and with all thy mind" (Matthew 22:37). We must love Him with our mind.

"Thou wilt keep him in perfect peace, whose mind is stayed on thee: because he trusteth in thee" (Isaiah 26:3). Pride trusts in itself, but perfect peace comes when one abandons human philosophy and trusts in the absolute law of God.

"Unto the pure all things are pure: but unto them that are defiled and unbelieving is nothing pure; but even their mind and conscience is defiled" (Titus 1:15). This is a philosophical war! "Absolute" (concrete) is pure and undiluted. It is easy to understand. The painting is clear; its parameters are well defined. "Abstract" is polluted. The painting is muddy looking, a haphazard mixture of colors without definition. Therefore, everything abstract is impure. The philosophical war is a war between the well-defined and the indistinct. The indistinct allows for worship at the unholy altar of humanism; the well-defined allows only for obedience to the supreme authority. You have a choice to make as to which philosophy will guide your life.

The battleground revolves around how faith is applied to fact. Faith is the evidence.

Life is an election. God votes yes, Satan votes no, and you cast the deciding ballot. The problem lies not only in the definition of facts but also in the application of faith. Faith is defined as "confident belief in the truth, value, or trustworthiness of a person, an idea, or a thing." The battleground revolves around how faith is applied to fact. A fact is "information presented as objectively real." Each person has a measure of faith, a certain capacity to believe. You must believe something!

The lowest level of human intelligence has certain paradigms that govern its activities. I can define the word "fact," but can I clearly define what is a fact? Indeed, fact requires faith. A person must decide in which set of "facts" he will place his faith. The abstract world thinks it has discovered some facts. I have no faith in their facts!

The courtroom stands in eerie silence as the Judge of all ages enters. He takes His seat and calls for the first case. A young Christian steps forward and begins to state his case: health problems, work problems, relationship problems. He continues laying the facts before the Judge until he is roughly interrupted: "Young man, I have not asked for facts."

"But you need to know what my problems are," the Christian counters.

"No facts are admitted as evidence in this courtroom!" His Honor replies. "Only faith is admitted. Please start again, but this time, state only your faith. The facts are of no consequence. 'Faith is the substance of things hoped for—the evidence!'"

The clash of ideas

In the philosophical war, evolution is a journey of random mutations (accidental changes) from somewhere unknown to somewhere else, also unknown. Do we want to build our world on a mere theory with no basis in fact? One may as well build a house upon the sand.

The reasoning goes round and round. If there is no Maker, then there is no moral standard. The strongest man is always right; it's the survival of the fittest. The winner makes the rules—until a stronger man comes to town. When that happens, refer to the beginning of this paragraph.

If there is no Maker, then there is no moral standard. The strongest man is always right; it's the survival of the fittest. The winner makes the rules—until a stronger man comes to town. When that happens, refer to the beginning of this paragraph. And so on . . .

The little hamster runs and runs, but his exercise wheel goes nowhere. When he decides he has arrived, he is in the same place where he began—a journey from nowhere to nowhere. Some call it life, but it is merely existence, and the rationale goes nowhere: if there is no God, then there is no me. If there is no me, then there is no you. I am not writing this book; you are not reading this book. "Ride a painted pony and let the carousel spin."

Jesus said, "I am alpha and omega." John wrote, "All things were made by him; and without him was not any thing made" (John 1:3). I like that. I have faith in that fact. The first four words of the Bible give me immeasurable comfort: "In the beginning God . . ." When I dig down to my roots, I find something solid—something concrete. The universe is orderly: everything runs like clockwork; everything remains in its place; everything functions for the purpose it was created.

The Big Bang vs. Creation

When worldly philosophers dig down, they find a big bang. They find that we are all riding on particles that are ever flying outward from the epicenter of the explosion. Abstract has no foundation or it would be concrete. What they call facts are not facts at all. This misguided generation has exalted human philosophy to the throne of God. Their agenda is to call biblical fact a theory and call the theory of evolution a fact. In which "fact" is your faith anchored?

"For ever, O LORD, thy word is settled in heaven" (Psalm 119:89). Settled? It's a settled issue. That's what I call a fact.

The concrete message says that God formed man of the dust of the earth. God breathed the breath of life into me and you! The abstract message says that a series of accidental explosions brought the proper elements together that created elemental life, which in turn evolved into life as we know it. If the concrete requires faith, then the abstract requires nothing short of wild imagination!

What really happened at Creation? There was only one there, and He's the One who wrote the book. I suggest that you read it. It is an all-time bestseller.

The Artist saw that it was good. He knew exactly what He had painted. I too know what He painted; I have been to the Garden of God.

The abstract message says:

(1) I came from somewhere indefinite.

> (2) I have no Creator; therefore, I answer to no one higher than
> myself.
> (3) I define my own morals.
> (4) I am going somewhere indefinite.

In other words, I have an indefinite origin. I have an indefinite guiding philosophy in life. I am going somewhere indefinite. Am I supposed to be comfortable with this?!

The concrete message says:

> (1) I am a creation of God.
> (2) He has given me distinct moral guidelines for life.
> (3) He has clearly defined my destination.

In other words, I know where I came from. I know how I am supposed to live. I know where I am going. I am very comfortable with this!

Madalyn Murray O'Hair, founder of American Atheists, dedicated her life to her message of atheism. She made it her life's goal to purge prayer from public schools, and she succeeded. She may have caused more havoc in the true church than anyone since the first-century man named Saul. O'Hair's ploy was possible only because Christians had been eating from the wrong tree.

David Waters, O'Hair's office manager, was a faithful student of her message, a wholehearted advocate of her dogma. If there is no Creator, then there is no moral foundation. If there is no moral foundation, then every man can do what is right in his own eyes. O'Hair had money. David wanted her money. Six years after her death, he admitted to killing her in a plot to steal $600,000 worth of gold. She was, in essence, murdered by her own message! She was buried in an unmarked grave at an undisclosed location. There was no prayer at her funeral. Her philosophy had taken her nowhere.

Genuine light vs. artificial light

I stand again before the canvas depicting the Tree of the Knowledge of Good and Evil. I must go behind the canvas again, for there is a fallacy that must be exposed. My soul takes me there.

I have told you of the serpent in disguise. The disguise is the serpent's philosophy; however, there really is no such thing as human philosophy. That leads me to tell you of the greatest treachery of all; few men are deceived by pure evil; instead, they are deceived by what looks good.

Be careful, lest that light in you is really darkness.

For such are false apostles, deceitful workers, transforming themselves into the apostles of Christ. And no marvel; for Satan himself is transformed into an angel of light. Therefore it is no great thing if his ministers also be transformed as the ministers of righteousness; whose end shall be according to their works. (II Corinthians 11:13–15)

The face of evil must be disguised to be effective. Would you be deceived by something as ugly and horrifying as blatant evil? Would you follow the serpent if you knew he was the embodiment of evil? It is the knowledge of good and evil that deceives. Most evil in history has been performed in the name of good. Many wars have been fought over religion, and most religion has the appearance of something good.

It is said that many cultures worship the same God; they just call Him by different names. But is my God really the same God as their god? If He were the same, His personality would have to be the same—but it's not. For instance, the god of some groups demands things of them that are incomprehensible—things like suicide missions. Their god foments hate, lies to his people, and presses them to act as judges of their fellow man. Conversely, my God compels me to give myself in love, for He so loved the world that He gave His only begotten Son. The judgment of my God is rooted in love; His love for righteousness causes Him to judge unrighteousness. His love for truth translates into a hatred for lies. Their god is not my God; their rock is not my Rock.

Even if my God were the same as theirs, salvation would still require the name of Jesus!

Peter, filled with the Holy Ghost, said unto them, . . . Be it known unto you all and to all the people of Israel, that by the name of Jesus Christ . . . doth this [impotent] man stand here before you whole. This is the stone which was set at nought of you builders, which is become the head of the corner. Neither is there salvation in any other; for there is none other name under heaven given among men, whereby we must be saved. (Acts 4:8, 10–12)

Do not be deceived by the pseudo "good" of world religions. Do not fall prey to the global ethic. This global ethic is not of human origin nor is it of religious origin. Its origin is the god of this world, and it is rooted in evil.

Woe unto them that call evil good, and good evil; that put darkness for light, and light for darkness; that put bitter for sweet, and sweet for bitter! Woe unto them that are wise in their own eyes, and prudent in their own sight! (Isaiah 5:20–21)

It has been said, "Other cultures are different: their eating habits and traditions are different, and they think differently. So it makes sense that their god would be different." However, let me remind you that Jesus was not an American citizen. But the truth of the God of Abraham, Isaac, and Jacob is the foundational Judeo-Christian truth of this country. The true global ethic had its origin before the "globe" existed. Do you remember the journey into the painting before Creation? We discovered that the "ethic" existed before the "globe." Godly culture existed before ethnic culture. Truth was settled in Heaven before there was an earth.

"Good" comes deceivingly. The root word for "humane" is "human." "Humane" means "characterized by kindness, mercy, or compassion; marked by an emphasis on humanistic values and concerns." I'm speaking of something beyond what humanity can accomplish. Humanity can do great things, but man cannot save himself. "That which is born of the flesh is flesh." The flesh cannot produce spiritual results.

"Good" can be deceptive

The entire community respected him. They knew he could not pass by a beggar without giving him money. There was not a more benevolent man in town. Charities could always depend on a generous donation from him, and when some poor soul was stricken *with disease and the neighborhood wanted to help, this man could be depended on to supply a great portion.*

It was also a known fact that he prayed and fasted often. If one passed by this man's house at the right time, he could hear a raised voice in communication with God. No person in town doubted the sincerity of this staunch citizen, and no religious man would have doubted his salvation.

Then an angel paid him a visit and uttered some shocking words: "Cornelius . . . your prayers and gifts to the poor have come up as a memorial offering before God. Now send men to Joppa to bring back a man named Simon who is called Peter." When Peter arrived, he preached the gospel to Cornelius and his house, and they all received the Holy Ghost and were baptized. What can be learned from this account? Cornelius did "good" (humane, benevolent) things, but he still needed true salvation. In the true scope of things, there is none "good" but God. Man can be humane, but man is not inherently good.

I am again behind the canvas of the Tree of The Knowledge of Good and Evil, learning the treachery of "good." "Good" tells people that all is fine when the blood of Jesus has not been applied. "Good" probably whispered to Cornelius that he didn't need to send for Peter as the angel had commanded. "Good" ignores doctrinal truth because those with another message are doing "good things." The deception of "good" will pull you off the foundation of truth, out of the Tree of Life, and onto the slippery slope of the abstract.

Eve saw the fruit was "good." Good for what? Good for deception. Good for getting her and Adam banished from the Garden. Nothing coming from Satan's tree is good! Let me assure you it is good only for the serpent and his cause. You are his pawn. You are deceived when you partake of his tree—not by evil as much as by "good"— good that is evil. Satan's tree is the tree of "good" and evil.

I return from behind the canvas wiser than before. From now on I will look behind the good to make sure that all that seems good is backed by truth!

> But as for me, my feet were almost gone; my steps had well nigh slipped. For I was envious at the foolish, when I saw the

prosperity of the wicked. For there are no bands in their death: but their strength is firm. They are not in trouble as other men; neither are they plagued like other men. Therefore pride compasseth them about as a chain; violence covereth them as a garment. Their eyes stand out with fatness: they have more than heart could wish. They are corrupt, and speak wickedly concerning oppression: they speak loftily. They set their mouth against the heavens, and their tongue walketh through the earth. Therefore his people return hither: and waters of a full cup are wrung out to them. And they say, How doth God know? and is there knowledge in the most High? Behold, these are the ungodly, who prosper in the world; they increase in riches. Verily I have cleansed my heart in vain, and washed my hands in innocency. For all the day long have I been plagued, and chastened every morning. If I say, I will speak thus; behold, I should offend against the generation of thy children. When I thought to know this, it was too painful for me; until I went into the sanctuary of God; then understood I their end. Surely thou didst set them in slippery places: thou castedst them down into destruction. How are they brought into desolation, as in a moment! they are utterly consumed with terrors. (Psalm 73:2–19)

The key part of any structure is its foundation. If the foundation is inadequate, the building will not stand. This can be applied to the philosophical war. All human philosophy is founded on the theories of human origin. All cultural mores and customs are based in human origin.

Have you ever been deceived by something that seemed to be good? Have you ever searched deeper and found it to be deceptive? If so, then we are on the same journey.

It is simple: either God is my Creator, or He is not. I know that He is, for I have been to the Garden of God. He has given me access to the Tree of Life and commanded me to avoid the other tree, which is a tree of "good" and evil. I am happy, for I am a concrete man in an abstract world.

❦

Questions swirled in Chad's mind as he walked the halls of The Art Gallery, searching for the Curator. The man had to be somewhere; he was always in the gallery. The Curator might have some answers. Why was he making himself scarce? Surely it would be easier if the Curator would guide him on his journey through The Art Gallery.

As he searched, a conversation with a guy named Mike, one of his coworkers at Circuit City, came to mind. Knowing Chad was a theology student, Mike had looked him in the eye and remarked, "I've been thinking. You and I were both raised in a predominantly Christian culture. I admit that I'm not as dedicated to religion as you seem to be, but I have a basic understanding of the principles that guide our faith."

Chad replied, "Yes, I believe you do. But God is seeking more than intellectual affirmation. God reveals Himself to us through His Word. And He expressed Himself to mankind in the life of Jesus Christ. Our faith rests on Him."

"But we were both raised in a Christian culture," said Mike, "so it's logical we would believe all of that. I'm just saying, maybe we should look at it more globally. For instance, take our computer geek—Ihsan. He's very religious. He's dedicated to his faith, much more so than most people who profess to be Christians."

"Oh, I agree he's very dedicated," said Chad. "I would never question his sincerity, but I can't embrace certain aspects of his theology. The Bible teaches that Jesus is the only way to salvation."

Mike pondered this, then asked, "But what makes our ideas about religion better than Ihsan's? He prays several times a day, and I don't do that. I don't even see you doing that."

Chad nodded, "It is admirable how often he prays, and I certainly will accept the challenge to pray more, but the One to whom we are praying is the most important thing. If I pray to someone who's not there, are my prayers really effective?"

"But Allah *is* there. Isn't Allah the same as our Jesus, just defined by a different culture?"

Chad was taken aback by this idea. Having been raised in a somewhat protected environment, he felt challenged by exposure to other ideas and beliefs. He should have known these kinds of challenges were inevitable, but he still scrambled for words to defend the truth he held so dearly. "Well . . . let me ask you this. What about all the terrorism in the world because of the beliefs some extremists of their faith have caused? What about calling everybody who doesn't agree with them infidels and believing they should be destroyed?"

Mike answered, "I admit some things in the Koran have been taken to the extreme, but Christians also have been known to take things in the Bible to the extreme. In any case, I know Ihsan is not a violent person. He would never do something like that."

Chad nodded. "I know Ihsan is a kind and peaceful person, but the religion he believes in can be violent. If his god is the same as my God, would not the personality of his god be the same as my God? It seems to me that his 'Allah' promotes hate, while my Jesus promotes love. His god asks his followers to die for the cause, while my God came to earth and died for me. I can't reconcile these two different natures as being from the same God!"

Mike retorted, "Then why are there so many religions in the world besides Christianity? Can they all be wrong?"

"My pastor says religion is man's attempt to find God; salvation is God's attempt to find man. Religion is man trying to define God; the Bible is God defining and revealing Himself to man. So although those other faiths may be called religions, they are really philosophies, and philosophies are of human origin, not from God."

Chad continued, "I remember a lesson Pastor Hanson taught us about Islam, saying Arab Christians were using the word 'Allah' for God prior to the dawn of Islam. But they were using it in the place of the word 'Elohim,' *and never in place of Yahweh or Jehovah.* Allah is a generic name never used to denote the personal name of God. I'd rather believe in the God of the Bible who had a specific, personal name. In the Old Testament His name was Jehovah; in the New Testament, the angel told Joseph to 'call his name JESUS: for he shall save his people from their sins.'"

"Well . . ." Mike seemed noncommittal, so Chad tried another tack, "The Koran says Allah forgives people when they repent, but they must never commit that sin again. But the Bible says in I John, 'If we confess our sins, he is faithful and just to forgive us our sins, and to cleanse us from all unrighteousness . . . And if any man sin, we have an advocate with the Father, Jesus Christ, the righteous.'"

Although Chad's words were genuine and spoken in sincerity, his heart was in turmoil. It seemed that his faith was being tested from every direction. His spirit was so troubled that after work that day he telephoned Pastor Hanson. Listening to important voices in his life would deflect the fiery darts of confusion the enemy seemed to be throwing at him.

Brother Hanson said, "Sure, Chad. You don't need an appointment to talk with me. Tell you what—why don't you come over right now?" When Chad arrived, the pastor ushered him into the dining room and they settled themselves at the table. From the kitchen Chad heard the coffee maker gurgling and the quiet clink of dishes and cutlery. Sister Hanson must be preparing one of her famous snacks! Chad's mouth watered. It had been a long day at school and work, and he was hungry.

Pastor Hanson asked, "What's on your mind, Chad?"

"Pastor, I'm glad you encouraged me to further my education at the seminary. But lately I seem to be facing a lot of questions, especially from the professor who teaches Religious Philosophy. Then today, I had a conversation with one of my coworkers about the validity of other religions. It seems there's a strong effort in our society to devalue the teachings of the Bible and embrace the other religions of the world that evolved from various cultures. While I believe that I'm strong in my faith, I sometimes don't know the most effective way to defend it. And I must admit that some of these ideas I've been encountering seem logical."

Sister Hanson appeared with a plate of sliced homemade bread and a platter loaded with meats, cheeses, and fresh veggies. On the table was an array of condiments, several kinds of pickles, and a large bowl of chips. Smiling, she handed Chad a plate: "You can build your own sandwiches. I'll go get the coffee. Or would you rather have soda?"

"Coffee would be great. Thank you!"

When she returned with the coffee, the three of them said a blessing over the food and began eating.

Pastor Hanson said, "You must first realize that only God can define truth. If you chase man's ideas, you'll always be chasing and never catching. Admittedly, there are good things to be said about the many religions of the world, but only the truth of God's Word can set people free."

"I know that and believe that, Pastor. So why am I so troubled and confused? There does appear to be strong cultural influences on religious beliefs."

"You've got to keep in mind that spiritual culture transcends all other cultures. Human cultures are manmade; spiritual culture is biblically based. It is defined by God, not by customs and mores of a particular society. Son, I'm telling you that your problem is also your solution. You have always been sincere in your quest for God's will. I trust your sincerity will not allow you to accept anything that is not valid, but it will also lead you on an exploration of all things. Sincerity causes you to listen to all of them, but sincerity also causes you to return to your trusted source for the final answer. Be assured that the people to whom you will someday minister will ask and be asked these same questions. Therefore, God has taken you on this journey so you will be able to help others. One cannot find answers until the questions are asked. But when your faith is tried, you must return to the true and trusted source, the Word of God."

"So," answered Chad, "God has led me to these questions so He can lead me to the answers. Thank you, Pastor! You've given me the answer key to all of my questions."

Pastor Hanson smiled. "One has to be convinced in order to be convincing. God is in the process of convincing you."

On the way home Chad realized he'd been wrong to search for the Curator of The Art Gallery when he had a question. The Curator knew it wouldn't be right to accompany him on his journeys behind the canvas; he had to go there alone. As the elder had said in his book, each seeker must have his solitary desert experience. Many men in the Bible like Moses, Elijah, John the Baptist, Jesus, and Paul had spent time alone in the desert so they could minister powerfully and effectively. He too must spend time with God in a private place in order to be equipped to display God's glory in a public place.

Chad was aware his friends were wondering why he'd been avoiding most of their times together, but he couldn't give up on the pursuit of the deep truths he was discovering. Even if stray ideas tried to pull him back to his friends, something stronger was urging him to persist in his search.

Chapter 7

The War Within

*T*he time has come for me to paint my own picture, now that I've seen the end of the journey. I hope I can do the painting justice, for it is a very difficult concept to express with art—this inward struggle of choice between the concrete law of God and the abstract world of human philosophy. It will be hard to portray the blood and guts, the anguish and tears involved in this struggle, and since there are degrees of revelation that contain little details, I will apply thick layers of paint on the canvas—a technique called "impasto." When dry, impasto provides a layered texture, and the paint will appear to be coming out of the canvas.

So, welcome to my drawing room. Pull up a chair and watch as I attempt to paint the inner struggle of the heart. The philosophical war that is raging in the world is nothing compared to this. The stakes of the war within the heart are very high. The heathen will always rage, but my concern is your personal battle. It would be impossible to cut down the Tree of the Knowledge of Good and Evil and forever silence its lies. The tree must live, for man must exercise his power of choice.

Choice! That is the war within. For now, you must fight your battle with self. Go look in the mirror and get acquainted with the one person that stands between you and Heaven. Great minds do battle atop the world's Mars' Hills, but the fate of your soul rides upon the battle within.

Are you comfortable in my drawing room? Here, have a seat in this nice chair. I'll warm up a cup of coffee for you. Are you ready for me to paint?

First, I must paint the curse. Not the curse of labor and sweat that falls upon all men. Not the curse of pain in childbearing and subjection that befalls all women. Not the curse of thorns and thistles that threatens the existence of your beautiful garden. Perhaps it is the thorns and thistles that were left in my heart.

When David wrote, "Behold, I was formed in iniquity, and in sin did my mother conceive me," he did not mean that the act of conception was sin, but the condition of his heart had been suspect since his birth. Like David, I came from a good home. I was blessed with wonderful parents. No one taught me to lie. No one taught me to steal. "Lust" was not a subject taught in kindergarten. Yet oh, wretched man that I am!

As a man bends a sapling to cause a deformity that will remain as the tree matures, so was my heart bent toward evil. I had within me the rage to rule. And rule I did, until I dragged the broken, deformed results to an altar of repentance. Then I surrendered the rule. Then I did it again. Then I did it again. As Paul said, "I die daily."

So this is the curse: "When I want to do good, evil is right there with me. For in my inner being I delight in God's law; but I see another law at work in the members of my body, waging war against the law of my mind" (Romans 7:21–23, NIV). Oh, that there was an off switch that would prevent my cursed nature from ever rising again. Today I know the truth, but will I know it tomorrow? They that enter the world of the abstract claim to have the truth. Of course, they cannot justify their claim with Scripture, but they seem convinced.

Could I also become convinced? Could I preach the gospel and still become a castaway? Gravity! The problem is the strong downward pull of gravity.

- *"Keep thy heart with all diligence; for out of it are the issues of life" (Proverbs 4:23).*
- *"The heart is deceitful above all things, and desperately wicked: who can know it? I the LORD search the heart, I try the reins, even to give every man according to his ways, and according to the fruit of his doings" (Jeremiah 17:9–10). Beware of your heart!*

- *"And GOD saw that the wickedness of man was great in the earth, and that every imagination of the thoughts of his heart was only evil continually" (Genesis 6:5).*
- *"But those things which proceed out of the mouth come forth from the heart; and they defile the man. For out of the heart proceed evil thoughts, murders, adulteries, fornications, thefts, false witness, blasphemies: these are the things which defile a man" (Matthew 15:18–20). Did you get a good look at the person in the mirror?*
- *"Take heed, brethren, lest there be in any of you an evil heart of unbelief, in departing from the living God" (Hebrews 3:12). You are the one that should take heed. Remember, seeds planted in the soil of the heart will one day produce fruit. You will be known by your fruit.*

The greater the mass, the greater the effect of gravity (i.e., the larger I am the more I weigh). The more carnality I allow in my heart, the greater the gravitational pull upon my soul. When the carnal mind is fed, it becomes stronger and begins to assert itself. Reason begins to rule over the Word. Questions begin to fly through the mind. What seemed concrete yesterday seems abstract today.

This is the war in my members. It is the war between my cursed fallen nature and the blessed new nature. God has established a beachhead in my soul, but the war for dominion still rages.

I cannot paint the picture quite as masterfully as Paul did. Perhaps you can comprehend the war by viewing his masterpiece.

For we know that the law is spiritual: but I am carnal, sold under sin. For that which I do I allow not: for what I would, that do I not; but what I hate, that do I. If then I do that which I would not, I consent unto the law that it is good. Now then it is no more I that do it, but sin that dwelleth in me. For I know that in me (that is, in my flesh,) dwelleth no good thing: for to will is present with me; but how to perform that which is good I find not. For the good that I would I do not: but the evil which I would not, that I do. Now if I do that I would not, it is no more I that do it, but sin that dwelleth in me. I find then a law, that, when I would do good, evil is present with me. For I delight in the law of God after the inward man: but I see another law in my members, warring against the law of my mind, and bringing me into captivity to the law of sin which is in my members. O wretched man that I am! who shall deliver me from the body of this death? I thank God through Jesus Christ our Lord. So then with the mind I myself serve the law of God; but with the flesh the law of sin. (Romans 7:14–25)

There is therefore now no condemnation to them which are in Christ Jesus, who walk not after the flesh, but after the Spirit. For the law of the Spirit of life in Christ Jesus hath made me free from the law of sin and death. For what the law could not do, in that it was weak through the flesh, God sending his own Son in the likeness of sinful flesh, and for sin, condemned sin in the flesh: that the righteousness of the law might be fulfilled in us, who walk not after the flesh, but after the Spirit. For they that are after the flesh do mind the things of the flesh; but they that are after the Spirit the things of the Spirit. For to be carnally minded is death; but to be spiritually minded is life and peace. Because the carnal mind is enmity against God: for it is not subject to the law of God, neither indeed can be. So then they that are in the flesh cannot please God. But ye are not in the flesh, but in the Spirit, if so be that the Spirit of God dwell in you. Now if any man have not the Spirit of Christ, he is none of his. (Romans 8:1–9)

This I say then, Walk in the Spirit, and ye shall not fulfil the lust of the flesh. For the flesh lusteth against the Spirit, and the Spirit against the flesh: and these are contrary the one to the other: so that ye cannot do the things that ye would. But if ye be led of the Spirit, ye are not under the law. (Galatians 5:16–18)

Perhaps I can paint something else for you that portrays a powerful influence on my actions: I have left a book feeling more liberal than when I began reading. I have left a conference feeling more liberal than when I arrived. I have left conversations with friends feeling more liberal than when I joined them. But I have never left an altar of prayer feeling more liberal than when I knelt. This speaks volumes, and I hope it paints a clear picture for you.

When the curse rages within, take it to the altar. When the flesh rears its ugly head, don't take it to the top of Mars' Hill. Instead, starve the flesh and force it to go to the altar. There you will be lifted up on the wings of your most holy faith, praying in the Holy Ghost! The battle will be won; your heart will be fixed.

"Shall not God search this out? for he knoweth the secrets of the heart." You cannot hide from God what is in your heart because it is plain for all to see in the fruit that is dangling on the branches of your tree.

So pray this prayer daily: "Let the words of my mouth, and the meditation of my heart, be acceptable in thy sight, O LORD, my strength, and my redeemer" (Psalm 19:14). Make sure the secret thoughts of your heart are acceptable in God's sight. Then you will not have to worry about the fruit dangling from the branches of your tree. How is this accomplished?

"Create in me a clean heart, O God; and renew a right spirit within me" (Psalm 51:10). Is He not the Creator? He can create a clean heart, and He will see that it is good!

How can you keep your heart clean? "Thy word have I hid in mine heart, that I might not sin against thee" (Psalm 119:11). You must make certain that you eat from the Tree of Life. Remember, the seed is in the fruit. The fruit you consume will determine the seed within you. When He creates a clean heart in you, and you hide His Word inside of it, then you can claim that your broken heart has been fixed—set aright, standing firm and upright. "My heart is fixed, O God, my heart is fixed: I will sing and give praise" (Psalm 57:7). Your heart is fixed and your mind is focused on the finish line. Your mind is made up. You are a concrete person.

When people are filled with the Holy Spirit of God, they have within them two natures. One is the fallen nature inherited from their father Adam. This nature likes to rule. But their new birth gives them a new nature that has power to rule if they feed it the right food. It was prophesied that the elder son, Esau, would serve the younger son, Jacob. Applied in a spiritual sense, this means the first birth becomes subject to the second birth! As many as are led by the Spirit of God, they are the sons of God.

My beloved, in the overall scheme of things, there is little you can do to help fight the philosophical war raging in the world, for the doom of this world has been foretold in the Scriptures. The church's day is not in this dispensation. I believe there is a revival of the concrete in the world of the abstract, but I do not believe the abstract will disappear or even diminish. Strong delusion must run its course to determine who really loves truth. Strong delusion will separate the wheat from the tares. The church will reach many hungry hearts with the truth that brings absolute freedom, but it will not obliterate the curse of this world. The world of the abstract will exist when the church is gone. But the Lord will have His day and He will share it with us. When the Day of the Lord comes, He will descend with thousands of His saints. The concrete will fall upon the abstract and win the war. Until then, heed my words.

Thus, I say the war you must win is not the global philosophical war, but the war within. Keep your body under subjection. Save yourself from this misguided generation. Save yourself from the person in the mirror!

Be a misfit according to this abstract world.

It is now time to leave my drawing room. Have I painted a clear picture? There are aspects of this painting that are unique to you or me, but those aspects are never abstract. There is a clear delineation between right and wrong. I hope you get the picture. After all, I am a concrete man in an abstract world.

❧❧

Feeling an urge to pray, Chad laid aside the old manuscript and fell to his knees, grateful he was alone in this inner chamber of The Art Gallery. He prayed, "Lord, I come to You with a sincere heart and a repentant spirit. Right now, I feel so sure of winning this war that I want to say I'll never be tempted or led astray by human philosophy. But, Lord, my humanity makes me susceptible to failure, error, and delusion. I know that within me lie the seeds of my own destruction—if I should ever allow them to take root. So now I'm asking You to create in me a clean heart and renew a right spirit within me. Place a guard on my mind that will keep me from ever following anything that is contrary to Your Word. Thank You for Your tender mercy and compassion; they are new and fresh every morning. Great is your faithfulness! And it is surely Your faithfulness that has brought me to this place."

He thought back to the time of his early calling when he was sixteen. After church that morning he had gone to Pastor Hanson, who had told him, "The best way to prepare yourself for ministry is by prayer and study. That's what makes a minister effective in the work of God."

Chad prayed, "Lord, I want my heart to be filled with the same pure desire to work for You as when You first called me. Please use me for Your glory, Lord. Make Your Word a lamp unto my feet and a light unto my path; keep me from straying after anything other than the truths You have so clearly shown me. And if I ever stray, remind me that Your ways are above my ways and Your thoughts are above my thoughts.

"If I should begin to depend on my own abilities, please remind me that it's not my words that will bring deliverance to people—it is Your words. I'm only a conduit of Your compassion and grace. Let me never become so arrogant as to think I can add to or take away from any of the truths found in Your precious Word. Instead, I now dedicate my life to learning more and more about You through the revelations You have given me through your written Word."

He concluded by praying the prayer from Psalm 19, which the elder had said should be prayed every day: "Who can understand his errors? Cleanse me from secret faults. Keep back your servant from presumptuous sins, let them not have dominion over me. Then I will be upright and innocent of the great transgression. Let the words of my mouth and the meditations of my heart be acceptable in your sight, oh Lord."

A fresh peace flooded his heart as he knelt in the quietness of the Spirit. He thought back over some of the things the elder had revealed about his own personal conflict: "I can't afford to lose this inner war, for if I do, I'll not be fit for the Kingdom. I can't lead others to victory in a war I haven't yet won for myself."

With fresh determination, Chad arose and turned to the next chapter in the wise elder's book.

Chapter 8

Things Settled and Unsettled

I have returned to *The Art Gallery*. What a place it is, a cross-section of life! By now you should have discovered *The Art Gallery* is a place of expression where mankind puts his moral codes and guiding principles on display. It is a place where man communicates with more than words and, in some cases, better than words could ever communicate. It is the gallery of life.

It may be a pulpit where pictures are painted week by week. It may be a think tank where people's minds are stimulated and renewed. It may be a front porch where coffee and ideas are shared. It may be at Grandma's knee as she sits in her rocking chair. It may be under Grandpa's favorite shade tree listening to the accumulation of years of experience. It may be at the university, where great efforts are made to form the mindset of society. It may be in the Bible class where great efforts are made to destroy that worldly mindset. We are all in *The Art Gallery*, and each person draws conclusions from the things he or she views.

These are not casual conclusions. It is not a simple undertaking. The artistic portrayals are not meant simply for the pleasure of the viewer. I tremble, for the pictures I draw may have a bearing on other people's eternal life. My conclusions could determine where they will spend eternity.

I return to stand before the infamous abstract painting that started me on my journey. It is a sad painting to me because I have seen friends disappear behind its canvas, never to return. I myself may go into the abstract artist's drawing room, but I will go behind *that canvas only to rescue one of my friends. My soul yearns for them. I come back to the abstract often, hoping to see one of them reappear with new wisdom in his eyes and new understanding in his heart. I yearn to walk in the Garden of God with one of my lost companions. "Adam, where are you?"*

I can visit the abstract a thousand times and get a thousand different interpretations of its expression. Of course, they are all correct, for by its very nature "abstract" is what it is to the viewer. The artist makes no commitment; he says absolutely nothing, but he says it masterfully.

Today is a new day. There are new viewers with new opinions. They are unaware that I am a frequent guest, for few of them make return visits. One time through life, grabbing all the "gusto" they can—that is their theme. One burger and a large fry to go—fast food for the soul. Take one look, experience the pleasure, then go on to the next painting. They never realize their hasty decisions have eternal consequences.

He was a very successful businessman. The long hours and hard work had paid off, and he was sitting in the lap of luxury. Ignoring the cries for help of the less fortunate, he mapped out a plan for his future: "I will build bigger barns! I'll store up wealth for the future, and take it easy the rest of my life with no more worries." It all sounded so good, but he made one mistake. He said to his soul, "Eat, drink, and be merry." Sir, you cannot feed fast food to the soul, for it will never satisfy.

I prefer to savor the aroma of slowly simmering steaks while sipping tasty drinks and sitting around the table with companions, enjoying good intellectual rapport and a waiter coming by to check on things. Such nourishing meals are vastly healthier for the soul than fast food. That is why I return often to The Art Gallery. I want to build on something solid. When I depart from the gallery for the last time, I must know where I am going and who will meet me there. I must hear Him say, "Well done, thou good and faithful servant." So, while others speed through life, I take time to savor. While they rush through the drive-through, I sit at the table and patiently wait for the main course.

Not that I am the epitome of patience. Anyone who knows me would laugh at the thought. However, there are some places that bring out extreme diligence in me. One of those places is The Art Gallery.

I am looking for something settled in an unsettled world. How can there be anything settled in the abstract? I know that some people's minds are like cement, all mixed up in a misshapen mass that is beginning to harden. But the world of the abstract does not allow for permanence. Indeed, it abhors permanence. If man's mind is so supreme, then why is he constantly changing it? Why does each viewer of the abstract have a different interpretation? And why do they all claim to be correct?

I will not enter the abstract world, for there is nothing to go into. People who go there enter a nebulous realm. They live without guidelines. They are moving toward uncertain destinations, and they want me to ride along. No thanks!

I like demarcation lines, even though I have at times pushed them to the limit.

I sat beside the tennis court, watching the two young men exchange volleys. The tennis court had well-defined lines, but without any judges there were still problems. Time and time again one man would whack the ball close to the line—too close for comfort. Time and time again the other man would lie and say, "Out of bounds!" He was definitely winning the match, but by spurious means. I prudently did not get involved, but the disdain of my heart said to the young man who was losing the game, "Son, you need to pick better friends. If he ignores this tennis court line, he will likely ignore other lines. You may be riding with him one day when he ignores the solid yellow line in the middle of the road. Then it will be too late to learn the value of a line."

I like lines, even when they are ignored. You may say, "If they are ignored, then why even have them?" Because lines define what is right and wrong, even when they are disobeyed. To the young tennis player, the line served a purpose: it made him lie! If there had been no line, he could have justified himself by saying, "It was close enough." But the line made him lie. He knew he was lying. He could say nothing to justify himself.

The world of the abstract does not provide lines. Instead, it has gray areas—zones where right and wrong, light and darkness, merge into an amorphous haze. In my lifetime I have watched the gray areas expand and the black and white areas retract. The gray areas are getting larger while the black-and-white areas are getting smaller.

Lines provide distinction. They will either make you live right or they will make you lie. "But the word of the LORD was unto them precept upon precept, precept upon precept; line upon line, line upon line, here a little, and there a little, that they might go and fall backward, and be broken and snared and caught" (Isaiah 28:13, NKJV). They may have been snared and caught, but at least there were clearly defined lines.

"He that is unjust, let him be unjust still: and he which is filthy, let him be filthy still: and he that is righteous, let him be righteous still: and he that is holy, let him be holy still. And, behold, I come quickly; and my reward is with me, to give every man according as his work shall be" (Revelation 22:11–12). The last chapter in the Bible cries for the concrete and decries the abstract. "Give me some clear lines, some absolute boundaries!" God will judge, but not according to our humanistic principles. Hey, Mr. Abstract, you will face a concrete judge one day! You will have a better judgment if you obey the lines!

Moses had been on the mountain so long that the Israelites thought their leader was dead. They formed a mob and accosted Aaron: "Come, make us gods who shall go before us; for as for this Moses, the man who brought us up out of the land of Egypt, we do not know what has become of him" (Exodus 32:1, NKJV). Aaron devised a solution. He told the people to collect all of their jewelry. He melted down the gold and with a graving tool he fashioned a calf. The next day they held a festival. They offered burnt offerings and peace offerings to their new god, and the people "sat down to eat and drink, and rose up to play." A famed Jewish rabbi notes that the word "play" here indicates the people committed acts of pagan worship, immorality, and even murder. Meanwhile, up on Mount Sinai, the Lord told Moses to go back down the mountain and confront Aaron:

> *Moses said unto Aaron, What did this people unto thee, that thou hast brought so great a sin upon them? And Aaron said, Let not the anger of my lord wax hot: thou knowest the people, that they are set on mischief. For they said unto me, Make us gods, which shall go before us: for as for this Moses, the man that brought us up out of the land of Egypt, we wot not what is become of him. And I said unto them, Whosoever hath any gold, let them break it off. So they gave it me: then I cast it into the fire, and there came out this calf. (Exodus 32:21–24)*

Observe carefully the formula for creating an abstract god.

> (1) *Always listen to the people. The people know what kind of god they want. People always create their gods in their own image.*
> (2) *Make certain that you do it in haste; do not wait on the true man of God to come off the mountain.*
> (3) *Collect things from the people that are valuable to them: gold, silver, jewels, philosophies, pet peeves, etc.*
> (4) *Throw the entire collection into the fire.*
> (5) *Worship whatever comes out. The result must surely be holy! You have created an abstract god.*

So strip yourself bare and worship at your abstract altar. But when the true man of God comes down the mountain with the Law, your nakedness will be exposed.

I stare at the abstract painting. It looks like the ocean—restless, forever moving, forever changing. No one has returned today. How can one return from nowhere? I heard a preacher say that they will return, and I want to believe it. Perhaps my painting will build a bridge for the people who have disappeared.

"You got caught in the vortex, didn't you? Run, little hamster, run until you get to 'nowhere,' the land where new discoveries create new opinions, new opinions create new mores, new mores create new discoveries, and new discoveries create new 'facts.' But someday if you are ready to return from nowhere, I will be here to help you."

I have a hero from history, Colonel Robert Gibbon Johnson. His bravery impacted my life.

Dr. James van Meeter, speaking in 1830 to a crowd in Salem, Massachusetts, before Robert Johnson attempted his daring feat, said, "This foolish colonel will foam and froth at the mouth and double over with appendicitis. All that oxalic acid in one massive dose, and he's dead. If the Wolf Peach is too ripe and warmed by the sun, he'll be exposing himself to brain fever. Should he by some unlikely chance survive that, I must warn him that the peach skin will stick to his stomach and cause cancer."

Heedless of the physician's warnings Robert Johnson persisted with his plan. He picked up a raw tomato (once known as the Wolf Peach) and ate it in front of a startled crowd of onlookers. They waited breathlessly for the brave man to keel over, but nothing happened.

Up to that day, tomatoes had been grown in the United States only as ornamental fruits because everyone was afraid to eat them. Tomatoes were called "Wolf Peaches" because of the writings of an ancient Roman physician named Galen, who referred to plants whose identities had never been nailed down. He described the tomato as a poisonous Egyptian plant with strong-smelling yellow juice and a ribbed celery-like stalk. Some even believed if they tried a tomato they would turn into a werewolf. Johnson, however, had traveled to South America, where he had eaten many tomatoes and found them to be delicious. Thus he set out to change the tomato philosophy in America. Today, thanks to my hero, the United States is the greatest tomato-eating country in the world. It is amazing how human philosophy changes!

There was a time when everyone knew the world was flat, but few people believe that today. Humans are fallible. They can be wrong. Let me share a secret with you. The Word of God is exactly the same as it was when it was written. "For ever, O LORD, thy word is settled in heaven." Take the unsettled if you must, but I'll take the settled.

Let's look at five definitions of the word "settled," according to The American Heritage Dictionary:

(1) "To put in order: arrange or fix definitely as desired, to put firmly in a desired position." The Word of God is settled; it is exactly the way He wants it to be. It doesn't need human input or alteration. God has firmly placed truth and morality in a desired position. His truth endures to all generations; what applies to one generation also applies to the rest. New revelations and discoveries will not change it. It is forever settled.

(2) "To restore calmness and comfort to." There is no comfort or stability in the abstract; it is like a house on a shifty foundation. When the owners go away for a day and return tomorrow, will their house be in the same place? The point is the abstract has no foundation; it is founded on a lie, and there is no substance in a lie. Stability and comfort come from something solid. The Word of God is forever settled on the Rock, Christ Jesus.

(3) "To cause to sink, become compact, or come to rest." This is a reference to the settling of a foundation of a building. Once it is totally settled, it will not move. The Word of God was totally settled in

Heaven before there was an earth. It will never move. "Upon this rock I will build my church."

Some scholars claim that the doctrines of the New Testament had to be perfected over several centuries following the death of John, the last living apostle. Why is there not a prophecy concerning this claim, considering that the New Testament is full of warnings of false prophets and false doctrines that will arise? Since when has the hand of man perfected that which God has made? "And if thou wilt make me an altar of stone, thou shalt not build it of hewn stone: for if thou lift up thy tool upon it, thou hast polluted it" (Exodus 20:25).

"And you, that were sometime alienated and enemies in your mind by wicked works, yet now hath he reconciled in the body of his flesh through death, to present you holy and unblameable and unreproveable in his sight: if ye continue in the faith grounded and settled, and be not moved away from the hope of the gospel, which ye have heard, and which was preached to every creature which is under heaven; whereof I Paul am made a minister" (Colossians 1:21–23). Do not be moved from the hope of the gospel you have heard. That is the only foundation you can safely settle upon. Paul said, "If I or an angel from heaven preach any other gospel, let him be accursed." (See Galatians 1:8–9). This foundation has settled all it is going to settle. It is concrete!

(4) "To conclude a dispute by a final decision." This is a legal term. Once something is settled, it is settled for good.

Why argue about Creation? It is settled. Why argue about holiness and righteousness? They are settled. Why ponder about the plan of salvation? It is settled. Why dispute about the identity of Jesus? It is settled. It was settled before the foundation of the world, as He is the Lamb slain from the foundation of the world (Revelation 13:8). One can reason within the guidelines of the Word, but one should never reason outside of those guidelines. The Judge has made the ruling and no further arguments can be presented. The case is closed. The dispute is settled in Heaven—forever!

(5) "To become clear by the sinking of suspended particles." This is a reference to the settling of particles in liquid. The particles that make it cloudy will sink to the bottom, making the liquid clear. Any cloud of confusion should have dissipated long ago. The Word of God is clear, concise, and to the point. Do not attempt to muddle it with human philosophy. It is without controversy. It is settled.

Why not reexamine all five definitions and ask yourself this question: "Is the Word of God a settled issue in my life?"

I turn away from the abstract painting. None of my friends have returned from behind the canvas, and it saddens me. I walk again to the painting of the Tree of Life. It is concrete, solid, settled. I will build my house upon it, for I am a concrete man in an abstract world!

ȣȣ

Chad walked into the school library and saw Nicole Freeman sitting alone, elbows on the table, her head in her hands, staring down at a textbook. He came up behind her and cleared his throat. "Ahem."

She turned abruptly and looked up at him. He saw that she'd been crying.

"Er, sorry if I startled you." He pulled out a chair and sat next to her. "Is something troubling you?"

She blurted, "Am I the only one who believes?"

"No, you most certainly are not!" He smiled and plopped a frayed manuscript on the table.

She sat there looking at it. "What's that?"

"Believe me, you could learn a whole lot more from this old book than from that textbook you're reading."

"Where did you get it?"

"At The Art Gallery."

"You mean that old place where you go almost every day?"

"The very same." An excited look came over Chad's face. "Perhaps you'd like to go there with me sometime. You might find it as interesting as I do."

Her expression changed from anxiety to eagerness, and he was surprised to hear her say, "How about right now? I could sure use some fresh inspiration."

Grinning, Chad picked up the manuscript, Nicole gathered her books and papers, and they left the library. They headed downtown and turned into Destiny Lane, finally coming to the place that had become so dear to Chad but still remained such a mystery to his friends. Entering the gallery caused a tingle of anticipation in Nicole and she sniffed appreciatively. "Smells like beeswax furniture polish. Even the floor is polished to a shine."

"The Curator always sees to it the place is spotless and ready for guests."

"There aren't many people here, though." Nicole's observation was punctuated by their echoing footsteps.

"There never are. But the few who come here are like me—they come often. No matter how many times I've been here, I always learn something new, even after I've studied the paintings several times."

He began leading her through the various displays. Nicole appreciated his enthusiasm but kept looking at him askance, thinking, "What's all this business about journeying behind the canvases? Seems a little on the strange side, to say the least."

Chad kept up a running commentary as they ambled through the various rooms in the gallery. "When I first came here, all I could see was the various art expressions, but now I understand this is a place where mankind puts his moral codes and guiding principles on display. At first you simply look at the art to behold its beauty and appreciate the skill of the artist, but if you keep coming, you get to where you can look into the art. I must warn you, though, if you're really seeking, you can get pulled in."

Nicole stood transfixed by the depiction of a beautiful garden, saying, "One picture, a thousand words."

Then they entered the area dedicated to abstract expressions.

"Coming in here helps you discover a major contrast: the world of the abstract has no clearly defined lines, while the absolute Word of God firmly establishes truth and direction. When I first came to this place, I was very confused by what Professor Clark had been teaching in Religious Philosophy. However, what I found here has confirmed what I've always believed about truth and reality."

Nicole looked at the walls crowded with framed abstracts. The nebulous shapes and garish colors clashed and bled into each other. "I understand what you're saying. I admit that I've been disturbed by the direction of the professor's teaching—as well as the conversations among our friends."

Sensing an open mind and willing spirit, Chad began telling her about the parchment written by the elder as he continued contrasting things abstract and things concrete. They left the area dedicated to abstracts and moved to a room in the left wing of the gallery that displayed a painting called *The Lighthouse*. The majestic structure rose high, founded upon a strong rock that projected into the raging sea. There was a certain comfort it its rugged beauty.

Nicole commented thoughtfully, "That painting reminds me of a hike we once took to the New Dungeness Lighthouse in Puget Sound. I was amazed as I looked at the structure that had stood there for more than 150 years, imagining how many ships' captains had been guided by its light and how many lives had been saved. I was privileged to spend a whole week at Dungeness Lighthouse working as a volunteer to help maintain the historic site."

"Then you can really relate." They stood taking in the scene until Chad remarked, "You may find it hard to believe, but I can sense this painting drawing me, as if something is pulling me in."

Nicole nodded. "I feel it too. Let's go in together."

Chad looked at her and said, "I'm sorry, Nicole, but as much as I'd like to, I can't go with you. It's something you must do by yourself."

A strange feeling came over Nicole as she felt herself being drawn into the painting, her first journey behind a canvas. Understanding what she was experiencing, Chad simply waited until she was once again beside him gazing into the framed art.

"Tell me what you saw."

"It was awesome! I could feel its strength and confidence. It was standing there with certainty and absoluteness. I could sense it saying that it was there to stay."

Chad nodded. "Once you've been behind the canvas you understand the contrast between the stability of the concrete and the shiftiness of the abstract. The things Professor Clark is saying indicate that to him truth and reality are unsettled issues. But I'm learning that truth is settled, as settled as the feeling one gets in this lighthouse."

"It feels so much more secure to believe in something that's settled," she answered. "I would hate living in a world where everything is always as shifting and restless as the ocean waves. Tossing aimlessly in such a world you can't see the dangers lurking beneath the surface. I'm glad God has provided a lighthouse to point the way to safety."

Chad suddenly asked, "Would you like to visit my church with me sometime? You'd begin to see the picture even more clearly. Pastor Hanson is a great man and a good preacher."

Chad was once again surprised to hear her say, "I would love that."

Nicole eventually left the gallery to go to work, leaving Chad alone. Feeling euphoric about Nicole's receptivity to the concepts displayed at The Art Gallery, he turned toward the refuge of the now familiar room, sat down at the old desk, and once again opened the beloved parchment of the elder.

Chapter 9

The Lighthouse

In the left wing of The Art Gallery, in the corner near the bay window, stands an easel with a beautiful painting of a lighthouse. It is situated on a majestic mountainside overlooking the sea, ready to warn ships away from danger with its bright light. I love lighthouses. I love what they symbolize. My soul takes me into the canvas and my spirit searches the wonderful truths hidden in the lighthouse.

Lighthouses have always attracted attention. Collectors line their curio cabinets with replicas of these majestic marvels. For centuries artists have been captivated by their posture and expression, and have attempted to capture this spirit on canvas.

Why this fascination with lighthouses? They are certainly not exciting places to visit. There are no fast rides, no thrilling shows, no fancy cuisine. The interior has no spacious rooms and no elegant décor. Perhaps it is the symbolism of a lighthouse that gives us comfort. Perhaps a lighthouse represents something concrete in an abstract world.

The old sailor had logged many hours, spending most of his days on the open sea. He had traveled the world and seen the sights from Singapore to the Hawaiian Islands. He had sailed around Cape Horn and had drifted in the Gulf Stream. He had fought for his life through hurricanes and tropical storms. He had run for his life from natives on uncivilized islands.

He had gone ashore to find cities totally changed, wrecked by storms since his last visit. He had seen governments topple, and once-friendly shores become hostile to the sailor from the sea. He had seen just how quickly changes can come to what seems to be a stable society.

Now he returns home after what was meant to be his last voyage. He looks forward to hours of relaxation and great conversations about the world perspectives of a man from the sea. Though he knows that he will miss the excitement and the adventure, he is certain that the time has come in his life to place his feet firmly upon mother earth. What he has worked for his entire life now stands before him with open arms.

But one thing comes between him and his dream. During the night the weather begins to change and throughout the day it becomes steadily worse. It develops into one of the worst storms of his sailing career, and at this moment he is not taking his retirement for granted. Indeed, there is an element of fear in his heart, an honest fear known only to seasoned seamen. It is the deep understanding that this ship could be lost at sea, that these sailors' feet may never again feel the solid shores of home.

The winds quicken, yet the rain, fog, and mist remain. He is disoriented and uncertain. Is he heading north or south? Has the wind caused him to head back out to sea? Has he lost all sense of direction?

His eyes search the darkness for any familiar sight.

Younger sailors, fresh from their boasts of bravery, begin to feel despair. They look to the "old salt" for solace, but they see the worry wrinkles on his brow. If the old man is afraid, then the danger must be real. He attempts to put on a brave front, but it is a halfhearted attempt.

His eyes again search the night for that glimmer of hope.

A mast breaks and men scramble to secure the ship. Havoc reigns as men rush about, attempting to stabilize the craft without being swept overboard.

The old man constantly searches for the horizon. It is somewhere out there. It has always been there. He cannot remember a day when it wasn't there. It has welcomed him home on many occasions. Will it be there to welcome him home after this last voyage?

By now the beach houses along the shore have been smashed to pieces. "If their inhabitants have not fled to safer places," he reflects, "then many of them have already lost their lives." Houses of pleasure are not designed to withstand the storm.

His eyes catch a familiar glimmer. Is it? It is! A sense of relief floods him. A smile issues from his soul. These old feet will once again feel the solid earth. This old ship will once again greet the harbor. The lighthouse will point the way one more time. To all sailors tossing on the sea of life, the lighthouse is a matter of life and death.

The lighthouse may be a novelty to some and a tourist attraction to others, but it was built for a purpose. The location was chosen wisely, and it was constructed as if the lives of men depended upon it—for they do!

Preacher, what are you building? Do you realize that the eternal lives of men and women are riding upon your decisions? Has this revelation driven you to an altar lately? What ground have you selected to build a lighthouse upon? Are you comfortable preaching your opinions while ignoring the Word of God? Have you ceased being God's delivery boy and become His advisor? Have you ceased preaching the Word and started preaching your own interpretation of the Word?

As a young man I drove into the city of my calling. The thought that I had a church to build frightened me. It also frightened me the first time someone asked me a pointed question about the Bible and I realized I could not send him to someone else for answers. Oh, how easy it used to be when I could say, "Go talk to the pastor about it." Now I am the pastor, and I must answer their questions.

I was alarmed the first time someone challenged my authority as the man of God for this assembly. But nothing frightened me more than when people accepted me as pastor and expressed total confidence in my leadership. That absolutely terrified me. If they should ever rebel against the truth, then I would not be held responsible. But what if I myself led them to hell? Oh Lord, let me never be a blind leader of the blind!

I must trust in a reliable source. "Thy Word is a lamp unto my feet and a light unto my path." I am not building a house of pleasure. I am not building a place of entertainment. I am building a lighthouse, and the eternal lives of men and women depend upon my work.

Therefore whosoever heareth these sayings of mine, and doeth them, I will liken him unto a wise man, which built his house upon a rock: and the rain descended, and the floods came, and the winds blew, and beat upon that house; and it fell not: for it was founded upon a rock. (Matthew 7:24–25)

When you run into the house you are building, do you find refuge or pleasure? There is pleasure in truth, but it is not carnal pleasure. In His presence is fullness of joy, but you must be in His presence to know that real joy. It doesn't advertise well, because the carnal mind cannot discern the things of the Spirit.

Many have tried to water down the message to make sinners feel more comfortable. But there's nothing a preacher can do to make a sinner comfortable in the presence of God. God doesn't want sinners to be comfortable in His presence. He wants them to be convicted. You can adapt your building to fit society. You can advertise, "Come as you are." But there is nothing you can do to make sinners comfortable in the presence of God. So if your sinners are comfortable, you're holding forth in a beach house that is built on shifting sand.

Sinners have always been welcomed in lighthouses. We have never demanded that they meet a certain dress code to enter the lighthouse, so why the sudden shift of emphasis to the come-as-you-are advertisement? It is actually saying, "We will not ask you to change; instead, we 're willing to change our views to conform to yours. Our mutability will make you comfortable, so go ahead and come as you are." The spirit of conformity has invaded our churches. I repeat, there is nothing a preacher can do to make a sinner comfortable in the presence of God. That very discomfort is his only hope for salvation! At Pentecost they were pricked in their hearts!

Someone must build a lighthouse! The restless sea of the abstract world is full of lost vessels searching for direction. There are no lighthouses to guide them away from the treacherous shoals. Proponents of the abstract point the lost vessels to everywhere and nowhere. They don't know which direction will take them to safety.

But the true lighthouse stands strong and solid, built upon a Rock, surviving the storms of the ages. When you see it, relief floods your soul. "I can make it home now! I know which way to go."

Inside the lighthouse stands the watchman. His job description is not complex—keep the light burning day and night! Never let it go out. You do not know at what hour it will be needed. Lost sailors and violent storms do not have schedules. So the beacon must shine continuously.

> *And the fire upon the altar shall be burning in it; it shall not be put out: and the priest shall burn wood on it every morning, and lay the burnt offering in order upon it; and he shall burn thereon the fat of the peace offerings. The fire shall ever be burning upon the altar; it shall never go out. (Leviticus 6:12–13)*

I return from behind the canvas reluctantly; it is hard to leave the lighthouse behind. Why? It has no creature comforts. It is a plain place bereft of attractive décor. But it is a place that comforts my soul. It is a place of safety. When the storms come, I know I am secure within its solid walls.

What are you building? How much of your time, money, and energy is dedicated to carnal pleasure? When your life's labor is finished, will you be standing in a lighthouse or a beach house?

Back in The Art Gallery I gaze at my own creation. I have built a lighthouse. When others tried to convince me to build a beach house, I climbed to the top of the Rock and dug deep to lay my foundation. When the sun was shining the people enjoyed the pleasures of the beach houses along the shore. But when the storm came, they looked for me, the keeper of the lighthouse, and I was there, a concrete man in an abstract world.

❦

Encouraged by the successful visit with Nicole at The Art Gallery, Chad thought it was high time he asked his friends to go with him. He found them eating lunch at the Campus Café. They made room for Chad at the table, and the waitress took his order. While they ate, he was able to steer the conversation toward The Art Gallery. "I know you've all been curious about why I go there so much, and I'd love to show you around sometime. Say, I'm going this afternoon. Why not come with me?"

Nicole said eagerly, "I'd like to go there again. It was an amazing experience." Chad smiled, thinking of their time together and how glad he was that Nicole was now attending church with him.

Lisa hesitated. "I don't know . . . just the thought of going there makes me feel uncomfortable. You've never quite explained what happens there, so I don't know what to expect."

Chad was surprised when John said, "Well, I'll go with you. In fact, let's all go. It'll be a chance to clear up the Art Gallery mystery." Chad thought, "Well, I've accomplished my goal of getting them to come—if for nothing else than to satisfy their curiosity."

They all trooped down Destiny Lane, and Chad was thrilled to usher them into the gallery. He was confident that Nicole was beginning to see things the way he saw them, but he was unsure of how his other friends would react. He was especially glad that John had agreed to come. He thought, "Maybe John will at last see the difference between the absolutes of God's Word and the abstract of human philosophy."

As he led his friends through the various rooms, Chad related his own discoveries in the Garden of God and his insights about the two trees. Lisa seemed enraptured, but Chad was disconcerted when she raved, "Now that's what I call a beautiful garden! I just love the way the artist displays those beautiful flowers and trees. I can almost smell the fragrance." Apparently, she hadn't heard a word of his explanation. She continued, "That gorgeous painting reminds me of the Butchart Gardens we toured during last summer's vacation to Victoria Island. We walked the paths for hours, and it was one breathtaking sight after another: the colors, the exotic plants, the bowers, the gardens with different themes, and even a dancing fountain that lights up at night."

Chad was a little impatient about her fixation with gardens. She wasn't comprehending any of the precepts being portrayed. "Lisa, you must look past the surface of these paintings to understand the message of the artist." He thought to himself, "I guess the Curator was right; not everyone will be drawn in."

They moved to the left wing of the gallery and entered a beautiful room with a bay window. Two paintings dominated the room, one titled *The Lighthouse* and the other *The Beach House*. After Chad pointed out the contrasts between the two paintings, Nicole said, "To me, the lighthouse painting shows us that anything of value must be built upon a solid foundation. Human reasoning can't create anything that solid."

Chad led them to the legendary painting of the powerful arm of God outstretched in Creation. He explained, "To me, the concept behind this painting is key to understanding the Bible. But I feel like Professor Clark is trying to sidestep that understanding by taking away our awe of our Creator."

Nicole added, "I agree. It's like he's attempting to put God on the same level as man, subject to man's intellect and reasoning. When I look into these great works of art, I see a God who is so much greater than man could even imagine. I see an immutable God whose Word never needs to be edited or altered."

John retorted, "Funny you should say that, because that's the 'God idea' I'm struggling with. In fact, I'm beginning to think it's the other way around; you two"—he nodded toward Chad and Nicole—"are the ones who are struggling."

Dan, ever the lighthearted, interjected, "C'mon, guys. I've enjoyed all I can stand of your debates. Anyway, what's the big deal? My philosophy is eat, drink, and be merry, for tomorrow we graduate."

Chad was relentless. "Someday, Dan, you're going to long for something solid on which to stand. Either that, or you'll just keep taking the path of least resistance. As for me, I didn't start this journey just to have fun."

"You're spending entirely too much time here," John declared. "Taking yourself way too seriously!"

Dan found his way back to the room with the paintings of *The Lighthouse* and *The Beach House*. To Chad it was clear the lighthouse was securely founded on the high rock beside the sea, while the Beach House seemed to be squatting on the sand not far from the water's edge. The former was a monument of strength and stability while the latter was a fragile building susceptible to crashing waves and violent storms. But it seemed Dan didn't see it that way. "I think I prefer the Beach House—it's a lot less austere, much more inviting. I can see myself having a lot of fun there, no major changes required."

Chad was thinking, "Dan's all about waiting until after graduation to get serious. But will he ever get serious? I'm afraid he'll never want to leave the good times and get down to business of impacting people's lives for eternity."

Chad was worried because John kept returning to the abstract painting. He would be devastated if his friends' visit to The Art Gallery backfired. He began to question the wisdom of bringing them here.

The words of David's testimony in Psalm 90 came to mind: "He brought me up also out of an horrible pit, out of the miry clay, and set my feet upon a rock, and established my goings."

"Nothing about that rock sounds shifty or abstract," he thought. "Why can't John see the value—the urgency—of choosing the absolutes of God's Word?"

As John, Dan, Nicole, and Lisa were leaving the gallery, John declared, "This place gives me the creeps. And today's visit was anticlimactic to say the least. I don't see why you made such a big deal about this gallery. No offense, but don't bother asking me to waste my time coming here again."

Dan chuckled, "I might come again—if you nag me enough times. But I'm with John; this place makes me feel a little uncomfortable. If only you'd lighten up a little. I'm tired of you driving us to change."

Lisa tried to soften her friends' criticism. "Don't pay any attention to them, Chad. They don't like The Art Gallery because it wasn't their idea to come here. I'm glad you asked me to come, and I enjoyed the tour. But don't expect me to commit to anything just yet. I need more time to think about it."

Nicole gave Chad a knowing look.

As the door closed behind his friends, Chad did some soul-searching. *What was my motive in asking them here? I've committed myself to a ministry call, but it seems I can't even influence my close friends. So what good did it do?* He purposely took time to settle things in his mind. *Still, the elder is right. I refuse to build a beach house. I can't help it if the people I invite prefer it there rather than climbing the rock to the lighthouse I'm building. The lives of the people who choose to follow me there will depend on my work. There's no greater feeling than knowing someone has seen my light and escaped the storm. Others may choose to seek the path of pleasure, but I want to get my thrills from making a difference in the lives of other individuals.*

"Oh God," he prayed, "someone's got to build a lighthouse. Let that someone be me. I want my life and calling to be a light and a haven for the lost and broken in this world. Help me to keep the light burning. Let me hold to the lifeline of truth so I can rescue people from the storm. I want to have something strong and solid to offer them."

Whatever else his friends decided to do, Chad was determined to remain committed to the principles he'd received at The Art Gallery. With the picture of the lighthouse firmly planted in his mind, the young preacher opened the elder's parchment to another chapter.

Chapter 10

The Beach House

There is a place where the unstable meets the stable, where the uncertain meets the certain, where the unsettled meets the settled, where the abstract meets the concrete. There is a Rock at the gates of hell, and the church of the living God is founded upon this Rock. It is a lighthouse that warns the sailors away from the treacherous shoals.

Then there is a place where the water meets the earth. It is a place of human pleasure. It is the beach.

The beach is at the very edge of the concrete. It is the place where human philosophy meets divine law. Many men have built their houses on this beach. Some desire to build upon the concrete yet stay as close to the abstract as they can get. But the beach is not the Rock, and a beach house is not a lighthouse. And the builder is not a servant; he is a hireling.

(For many walk, of whom I have told you often, and now tell you even weeping, that they are the enemies of the cross of Christ: whose end is destruction, whose God is their belly, and whose glory is in their shame, who mind earthly things.) (Philippians 3:18–19)

I cannot discredit his talent, for the artist has painted well. Everything in the picture is very alluring. The beautiful blue waters are rolling onto the beach. The white sands welcome all pleasure lovers. The boardwalk promises many hours of fun. The beach house advertises a place to go in and rest. It is a masterpiece. I go into the canvas.

It is different here than in the lighthouse. The lighthouse may not be pretty inside or out, but it is strong and solid. Its builder knows that lives depend on its stability. It shines continuously. Conversely, everything about the beach house speaks of pleasure. Not the pure pleasure of God's presence, but worldly pleasures. I must admit that it entices even the concrete man. Is this not why the beach house was built? Is a beach house as good as a lighthouse? Is it possible to have both the concrete and the abstract?

We know that we cannot mix the concrete and the abstract. We know that the Tree of Life and the Tree of the Knowledge of Good and Evil are incompatible. One cannot partake of both. But is it possible to build on the concrete and remain very close to the abstract? Could I build on the beach?

There is a stark difference between the rocky shores and the smooth beach. The Rock stands strong and sturdy as a monument. Abstract waters beat relentlessly against it, but it refuses to move. The roar of the clash can be heard for miles, but the Rock stands firm.

However, the beach is part of both worlds. It holds a form of godliness but denies the true power of God. The sands from the abstract sea wash up on the concrete shore, and create a world that is part of both. The beach is where water and land merge, where solid and liquid unite, where abstract and concrete marry and (as the Old Testament prophet said) produce strange children (Hosea 5:7). These children bear resemblance to the concrete, but they have the nature of the abstract. Their doctrines appear to be founded upon the Word, but they have the distinct smell of paganism. The sand may rest upon the land, but the sea controls it. Its ever-shifting form relates more closely to its abstract father than its concrete mother.

It all begins with simple logic. Why build in some isolated place, such as the Rock? Why climb its jagged slopes, dig into the solid rock, and build where the masses of people never wander? Surely God wants us to build where the people are. The crowds gravitate to the beaches. Isn't that where we should be? It makes sense to me.

Eve saw the fruit was good for food, pleasing to the eyes, and a tree to be desired to make one wise. But though the choice seemed obvious and right, in the end it led to death.

Most calamities begin with simple logic. Remember logic is the fruit from that other tree. Logos is the fruit of the Tree of Life; logic likes to pass judgment on logos.

And so the workmen are called in and construction begins. Let's get a little of both worlds. Build it on the sand, at the place where abstract and concrete come together. This is where the crowds are.

Of course, they should come as they are. God forbid that any mention of change should interfere with our quest to draw the crowds. Let's not offend them with any demarcation lines, standards, or doctrines. Paul said he became all things to all men that he might win some. Taking that reasoning to the ridiculous extreme, does that mean we should become alcoholics to win alcoholics? No, one must remember that the only thing that attracts pleasure seekers is pleasure. Abstract abhors concrete, so human reasoning says in order to keep them we must feed them abstract. We should preach grace with no strings attached. We should preach a Calvary that doesn't change man but simply redefines sin. We should preach a Christ that came to earth just to make our sins permissible: "Repent and be baptized for the permission to sin!" Reasoning says, "Do not preach anything as concrete as righteousness and true holiness. They will turn away. Instead, feed them abstract and they will come!"

It may have started innocently enough, but now we find ourselves preaching vague messages that do not require change or commitment. Then self-justification changes the commandments into suggestions. Then logic convinces us those suggestions were for people back then.

Wait a minute! It is abstract, not concrete, that changes with the days. Concrete remains the same. Abstract preachers are getting sand in their eyes; sand that has washed up from the abstract and been deposited on the shores of the concrete. Beach houses are full of preachers with sand in their eyes. They advertise concrete but their mouths deliver abstract.

Do I sound like a broken record? I hope so. I hope the message echoes and reechoes in your mind until you understand. If you merely want a crowd, build a beach house, but you had better be prepared to feed them what they desire.

Before you gloat in your increasing numbers, I have seen more than a few crowded lighthouses in my day. But there is a distinct difference between a transient thrill and true, lasting joy. A difference between entertainment and true praise and worship. A difference between scratching their itching ears and preaching a gospel that will save their souls. I am convinced that there is a sea full of lost sailors looking for a lighthouse. They have tired of the cheap thrills of the beach houses and are searching for something that will save them. I am a revivalist that wants to see the church grow, but I am convinced that people will come to the Rock. I do not have to build on the sand. I will shine my light for lost sailors upon the sea searching for a way home!

From inside the beach house, behind the canvas, I gaze out upon the water. The mystery of the sea has always drawn man.

> *They that go down to the sea in ships, that do business in great waters; these see the works of the LORD, and his wonders in the deep. For he commandeth, and raiseth the stormy wind, which lifteth up the waves thereof. They mount up to the heaven, they go down again to the depths: their soul is melted because of trouble. They reel to and fro, and stagger like a drunken man, and are at their wits' end. Then they cry unto the LORD in their trouble, and he bringeth them out of their distresses. He maketh the storm a calm, so that the waves thereof are still. Then are they glad because they be quiet; so he bringeth them unto their desired haven. Oh that men would praise the LORD for his goodness, and for his wonderful works to the children of men! Let them exalt him also in the congregation of the people, and praise him in the assembly of the elders. (Psalm 107:23–32)*

The waters are unstable. Sailors go forth and soon encounter the storm. The waves surge into the heavens, then dive down to the depths of the earth. Their souls melt with fear as they reel to and fro like drunken men. They are tossed around in the world of uncertainty. They cry unto the only One who can save them from this abstract world of uncertainty. He brings calm into their world. Oh, that men would praise Him for His greatness!

If you are tossed upon the stormy waves of the abstract, there is hope! There is One who can bring stability to your world.

> *And straightway Jesus constrained his disciples to get into a ship, and to go before him unto the other side, while he sent the multitudes away. And when he had sent the multitudes away, he went up into a mountain apart to pray: and when the evening*

was come, he was there alone. But the ship was now in the midst of the sea, tossed with waves: for the wind was contrary. And in the fourth watch of the night Jesus went unto them, walking on the sea. And when the disciples saw him walking on the sea, they were troubled, saying, It is a spirit; and they cried out for fear. But straightway Jesus spake unto them, saying, Be of good cheer; it is I; be not afraid. And Peter answered him and said, Lord, if it be thou, bid me come unto thee on the water. And he said, Come. And when Peter was come down out of the ship, he walked on the water, to go to Jesus. But when he saw the wind boisterous, he was afraid; and beginning to sink, he cried, saying, Lord, save me. And immediately Jesus stretched forth his hand, and caught him, and said unto him, O thou of little faith, wherefore didst thou doubt? And when they were come into the ship, the wind ceased. Then they that were in the ship came and worshipped him, saying, Of a truth thou art the Son of God. (Matthew 14:22–33)

Jesus defied the abstract when He walked on it. He did it to prove His supremacy, but He did not habitually walk on the water. The command was to go to the other side. It is His will for us to go to the concrete. Once delivered, find something solid on which to stand!

I have been saved from the sea. Why should I want to dive under its waves once again? From inside the beach house I get an uncertain feeling. The entertainment is good for a while, but I see clouds gathering on the horizon. The wind is picking up. The waves are beginning to roll in and I feel the beach house shift on its shallow foundation. I do not feel safe here. I follow after the wisest people who leave in search of a more settled place. As we go, we encounter others still running to the beach house, thinking it will protect them. But I am not deceived, for I have been in the lighthouse. These houses of pleasure are not built to withstand the storm.

And every one that heareth these sayings of mine, and doeth them not, shall be likened unto a foolish man, which built his house upon the sand: and the rain descended, and the floods came, and the winds blew, and beat upon that house; and it fell: and great was the fall of it. (Matthew 7:26–27)

I must escape from behind this canvas. This is not a safe place to be. I could have stayed in the lighthouse forever and felt secure, but there is a certain element of fear in the beach house.

Why did the builder choose a spot as close to the sea as possible? Why did the pastor build his church as close to the world as possible? When did the preaching of the Word become the projection of personal opinion? When did the choir quit praising Jesus and start pursuing the art of entertainment? When did our praise services abandon participation and encourage observation? When did praise evolve into applause? When did this spirit of the abstract weasel its way in? When did we get sand in our eyes?

The sand may be a part of the land, but it comes from the sea, and the sea is constantly changing it. The Rock remains the same no matter what the sea does. I must build upon the Rock.

I gaze at the other people seeking shelter from the storm. I could call out to them; I could tell them it is safer in the lighthouse. But they would not hear, for I am just a visitor from the other side of the canvas. They do not know I am here, for they cannot see me. I cannot stay. There is no stability in a beach house.

What about you, my friend? Have you got sand in your eyes? Have you been tempted to abandon the straight and narrow to pursue a more popular course? Will the house you are building withstand the storm?

I stand again in The Art Gallery wondering about the fate of those caught in the storm. Finally, I can stand it no longer, so I turn and walk away. I walk back to the left wing of the gallery, to the corner near the bay window where the beautiful painting of the lighthouse stands steadfastly on the easel. I go in to wait out the storm, for I am a concrete man in an abstract world.

❧

As Chad finished reading the chapter on the beach house, his mind was on Jerry Dotson. He'd known Jerry a long time, as Jerry had once been his youth pastor. A few years back Jerry had, with Pastor Hanson's blessing, planted a church in the neighboring community, about a thirty-minute drive from Pastor Hanson's church. The two churches had, at least in the early years, enjoyed close fellowship, and Pastor Hanson had been a valued mentor to Jerry.

But over the years Jerry had grown impatient with the slow rise in attendance. He had become impatient with Brother Hanson's approach; he began labeling his former pastor's ideas as archaic, out of touch with postmodern society. He had discussed the problem with friends closer in age, and had begun incorporating their ideas into his church growth plan. Jerry wouldn't have described the changes as sacrificing doctrinal purity for public acceptance, but in Chad's mind that's what it boiled down to. He once had approached Jerry with his concerns, but Jerry simply dismissed certain scriptural passages as pertaining to another time period, or attempted to justify these omissions by referring to other passages that were challenging to understand. The end result was the same—he and his followers left the old path, believing they were enlightened.

Many who knew Jerry Dotson had been impressed with the initial surge in attendance, but a close observer, like Pastor Hanson, saw there was something lacking in the newer members. Jerry's come-as-you-are policy, at first referring to dress, had come to mean that no real change would be required after conversion. Thus, once in the church, the new members' lifestyles, behavior, speech, and dress were the same as they had been before they came to Christ. Brother Hanson grieved over the fact that this no longer seemed to matter to his friend Jerry.

A few years back Chad and his buddy John Foster had discussed the changes Jerry was implementing. Even then, John had shown signs of being drawn in by the progressive ideas. However, with the guidance of a strong and biblical leader, Chad had maintained steadfastness in truth. Chad thought about the elder's words in the parchment. They seemed to be expressing the train of thought taken by Jerry and others like him: "I must admit a beach house could entice even a concrete man. After all, isn't this why beach houses are built—to be more easily accessible to attract the crowds? Isn't it better to build on the beach than in an isolated, rocky place, where people have to climb jagged slopes and dig into the rock? I think a beach house is as good as a lighthouse—and certainly more effective when it comes to church growth."

During their discussions John had said, "Maybe it's possible to have both the concrete and the abstract. Isn't that what Jerry Dotson is doing?" Chad hadn't wanted to start an argument with John, but he knew it wasn't possible to mix the concrete and the abstract.

As time passed, Jerry began sacrificing leadership standards for a higher degree of talent. At first it was with the idea that he would train his leaders and develop their strengths, but what actually happened was he slowly began altering his position, requiring less and less from his leaders.

Pastor Hanson, Chad's mentor, had taken a different approach. He had been lenient with new believers and had shown mercy in the areas of leadership, but he never let his definition of spiritual maturity waver. In the end, he had held to the biblical principles and put the conversion of people over the growth of the congregation. Ironically, both growth and development had occurred.

It all began to make sense to Chad: **The sand may be a part of the beach, but it comes from the sea, and the sea is constantly changing it.** Chad thought, "Jerry Dotson has sand in his eyes. He's become more concerned with making people feel comfortable than rescuing them from the bondage of sin. Somewhere spirituality gave way to entertainment, and the whole concept of church growth became clouded. What began as a conversion model digressed into an attraction model. The goal became the way to 'attract' more than the way to 'convert.'

"That's what's been troubling me as I sit in those philosophy classes day after day. Abstract people like Professor Clark and Jerry Dotson can't see clearly because of the sand in their eyes. They promote keeping their religious affiliation while adapting it to the trends of the world around them. They're trapped in a house of their own building, trapped in something that will never ride out the storm of the last days. I'll choose the lighthouse any day." Encouraged, he turned to the next chapter in the parchment.

Chapter 11

The Parable of the Postman

It had been a dream that had followed him since childhood; as far back as he could remember, he had been mesmerized by the uniform the man wore. Every day he stationed himself by the front window, watching the postman work his way down the block. He knew that one day he too would be a postman.

All of his family members knew he felt a certain calling on his life and bought him gifts for Christmas and birthdays that conveyed this knowledge: little mail trucks that ran the roads in the carpet from dining room to den, little toy postmen that made the rounds every day. To the young lad, superheroes like Superman, Batman, and Spiderman always ranked second place to the highest calling in life—the man that carries the mail.

As the lad grew, he knew he must be careful about the source of his calling. He couldn't receive it from grandma, his aunts and uncles, or even his mother and father. He had to know in his own heart that he was called to be a postman. If he was convinced of this, it would motivate him to deliver the mail through rain, sleet, snow, hail, or any other deterrent he faced. It would give him the courage to deal with the dogs that waited for a chance to rip the seat out of his prized uniform. So although he grew into adulthood with an open mind, he knew in his heart that he was destined to be a postman.

He was determined to be at the top of his class, for he knew that only the highest achievers would qualify for the job. His childhood dream pushed him through his adolescent years; he saw himself delivering the mail, bringing joy to thousands as he faithfully brought long-awaited news to their doorstep.

The postman is the vital link between the communicator and the recipient. No matter how valuable the message contained in the letter, if it does not reach its proper destination, it is of no use. This is the role of the mailman. He provides a vital community service. It is imperative that he is smart enough and alert enough to deliver the right message to the right place at the right time. Failure to do so will certainly cause problems.

Mrs. Johnson's check must not get lost in the mail. She depends upon its prompt arrival. She will suffer if it is even one day late. Mr. Sandifer's interest statement from the mortgage company is important. He needs it to claim a deduction on that year's income tax. John Collins needs his Wall Street Journal. He is concerned about the economy and how it will affect his investments. Janet's letter from her soldier fiancé must be delivered. Communication with loved ones is vital to military morale. The postman has a very important job. While he is but one link in the chain of communication, he must make certain he does his job well. People are depending on him.

His day finally comes. He graduates at the top of his class. His application for employment falls into the right hands. The proper channels are gone through, and he stands in the class of new recruits, carriers of the mail. Smart, alert, faithful, persistent, and determined young people stand before the instructor for the final preparations. A lifelong dream is about to be fulfilled; he is about to don the uniform he has dreamed of since he was a child.

There is one final stipulation: the postman is never to tamper with the mail. His job is strictly that of delivery. He does not write the letters; he delivers the letters. He does not edit the mail; he simply brings it to its proper destination. It is a crime to tamper with the mail. Not only would that bring personal disgrace, but it could put him behind prison bars, a horrible end for such a noble dreamer. But no one needs to worry, for this young man is sincere. He has not chosen his occupation lightly. He knows within his heart that his higher calling is that of a postman. He was born to deliver the message.

Only Heaven can reveal the many faithful years he served his fellow man. He gave of himself without any ulterior motive. Only God could clock the miles he walked and the personal suffering he endured. When others called in sick at the slightest of ills, he donned his uniform and made his faithful trek. He would not relegate his job to a substitute, for this postman took his job seriously. The mail would be there rain or shine, sleet or snow, fair weather or foul. "Deliver the mail, in season and out of season . . ." He did not waver though there were times of monotony and repetition. The neighborhood knew him as a friend, a trustworthy postman to be cherished.

There were the daily talks with the elderly people that met him at the mailbox. Rising young businessmen would wave at him as they drove by on their way to work. And what thrilled him most was to see the young children staring out of the living room windows. He would always wave and smile and imagine them going to their toy mail trucks and making their daily rounds. It was good to have a position that was highly respected in the neighborhood.

But one must beware of misplaced compassion. Very serious problems can evolve from very innocent mistakes. His downfall began with Mrs. Johnson. The poor soul was struggling with her bills, and her monthly pittance left her financially destitute. On many occasions the postman stopped to listen to the precious lady as she spilled her sadness before him. Many a day he wished he could do something to help her. It was this compassion that began his downfall.

Please do not interpret this as an assault upon compassion. No one could have greater compassion than the Postmaster General. He was willing to send His only begotten Son into the world to assure that the message was properly delivered. Compassion is a wonderful quality in a postman, but blind compassion is good for no one. Truth is the greatest delivery one can ever make, regardless of whether the news is joyful or painful. Compassion should never cause a postman to tamper with the mail.

It all began with a letter addressed to Mrs. Johnson. Knowing her distress, he struggled with the temptation to put it in the dead letter section of the post office. He couldn't make a good decision if he didn't know what the letter contained, so, overriding the strong allegiance to true values, he steamed the letter open. The message said, "Will a man rob God? Yet ye have robbed me. But ye say, Wherein have we robbed thee? In tithes and offerings. Ye are cursed with a curse: for ye have robbed me, even this whole nation. Bring ye all the tithes into the storehouse, that there may be meat in mine house, and prove me now herewith, saith the LORD of hosts, if I will not open you the windows of heaven, and pour you out a blessing, that there shall not be room enough to receive it."

He mulled over what he should do. He had faithfully delivered the mail for years, but he had just done something that signaled the beginning of the end—he had tampered with the mail. Surely the Postmaster General would understand. This was a unique situation. So he took his pen and scribbled a little note saying, "Mrs. Johnson, please do not feel you have to obey your obligation to the church this month. I know you are experiencing difficult times, and you could use that 10 percent to pay the unexpected hospital bill you received last week." He signed it and placed it in her box. In all his years of delivering the mail, he had never taken it upon himself to alter the message. He had always known he was just the postman.

Mrs. Johnson had faith in her postman, as all people should. When she read his note, it was as valid to her as if the author of the biblical letter had written it himself. What a pity, for two precious people had now started down the road of deception. The postman had crossed the invisible line that no mailman should cross, and Mrs. Johnson had shut the door to the blessings of God that had been keeping her afloat for years. Oh, what a crucial role the mailman plays! What a pity, for there were ways he could have helped the dear lady that did not require breaking the law.

Once the line had been crossed, it became easier to cross it again. Abstract was beginning to overtake the concrete; strange things were being justified by misplaced compassion.

A letter to Jill Wilson contained guidelines on how she would have to dress to qualify for promotion to a new job position. She was struggling with the decision because she believed they bordered on being immodest. The postman thought, "I can handle this. Surely the Postmaster General will understand this is a unique situation. Besides, she will be able to give more to the church with her pay raise." The tiny seeds of situation ethics that had fallen into the heart of the once-faithful postman had germinated and were now sprouting. Once he had only delivered the mail; now he was editing the mail. "It's OK," he told himself. "God understands." (Yes, God does understand!)

Then there was the letter that went out to everyone on the route. It simply stated, "You must be born again!" It used to be easy to deliver that message, but misplaced compassion and human reasoning had corrupted this once strong heart. Perhaps he had grown weary of the fight. Perhaps the years of faithfulness without spiritual respite were taking their toll. One thing was certain: Satan could do a lot of damage in the life of one who had earned the respect of the people. In five minutes he could tear down the ministry of a lifetime. Beware, Mr. Postman; don't betray the people's trust!

Still, he reasoned, "Why deliver such a letter? Mr. Sandifer hasn't been born again, but he's just as good as everyone else on the block. John Collins is so busy he can't be in church, but surely God understood the man works the swing shift. The mailman found it impossible to deliver the message exactly as written, so thousands of letters were discarded, letters that would determine the eternal life of the intended recipients. But they weren't worried because they had known the postman for years and trusted him. If he said something was unimportant, then it must be so.

Where was the honesty and integrity of his youth? What had happened to the proud young man who received his commission, never dreaming he would one day cross the invisible line? If someone had suggested back then that he would tamper with the mail, he would have considered it the greatest of insults. Yet now he sleeps at night, heedless of the fact that he is committing a horrible crime.

He gets sloppy. Those who are not easily deceived begin to notice a difference. They are not receiving as many true messages as before. It seems that now their mailboxes are stuffed with junk mail: buy-on-credit offers that are easy to get into and hard to get out of; get-rich-quick schemes; challenges about positive thinking; cheap grace; easy believism. The mail looks nothing like it used to. Some secretly begin to suspect the once-faithful postman has begun tampering with the mail. There is nothing to do about it but to appeal to the Postmaster General.

The Postmaster General knows. One day all postmen must stand before him. What a sad day for our mailman! Is there no reward for the many years of good service? Can one who has delivered the mail for years become a castaway?

Postman, your compassion for mankind must not make you blind to the truth. Regardless of what human philosophy is screaming in your ear, the greatest thing you can do is to deliver the truth just the way it is written. Never violate the postman's code. To do so is to exalt oneself above the Author of the letter. You must trust Him to know what is best. You must never violate His message by applying your intellect and reasoning.

It is indeed a sad story. The postman's dreams now lay in ruins. A lifetime of planning had swirled down the drain. His day of reckoning was upon him. He felt ashamed when he recalled the commission that had begun his career:

> *I charge thee therefore before God, and the Lord Jesus Christ, who shall judge the quick and the dead at his appearing and his kingdom; preach the word [deliver the mail]; be instant in season, out of season; reprove, rebuke, exhort with all longsuffering and doctrine. For the time will come when they will not endure sound doctrine; but after their own lusts shall they heap to themselves teachers, having itching ears; and they shall turn away their ears from the truth, and shall be turned unto fables. (II Timothy 4:1–4)*

Now he stands before the Postmaster General. He is ashamed of his error. He is stripped of his calling. His lifelong dream lies in shambles at his feet. He faces the people he deceived, dreading their vengeance. The blind has led the blind, and now both are in the ditch.

Such is the sad parable of the postman.

Have you ever been tempted to soften the message? Have you ever felt the need to make some slight alterations in the commandments? Grace is a marvelous gift, our greatest message. But is obedience becoming an antiquated topic? May God give us grace to be obedient!

Some pictures can be painted only with words. It is time to return to The Art Gallery. My heart is dragging and my soul is weeping for my friends that disappear into the abstract. Will I ever see them again? Is there hope for the fallen postman? Alas, I am a concrete man in an abstract world.

☙❧

The week before spring break, Chad walked into Pastor Hanson's office and settled himself in a chair. "You wanted to see me, Pastor?"

Pastor Hanson looked at the promising young minister and said, "Yes, there's a seminar being held by our state leaders designed especially for young ministers. Considering the things you've been struggling with at the seminary, I think this seminar is exactly what you need. If you can get off work in order to attend, I'll even pay your way."

"Oh, thank you! I'd love to go to the seminar, but when is it scheduled?"

"Next week—Thursday, Friday, and Saturday."

"Great timing, as that will be during spring break. I'll see if my boss will let me off work next Thursday and Friday and I'll get back to you."

The three-day seminar turned out to be one of Chad's most treasured memories as elder after elder poured into him the principles of ministry. Some of it had been hard to swallow, but he knew the things he was hearing were firmly establishing him for the call God had placed upon his life. He had been taught homiletics; he had learned the difference between eisegesis and exegesis. He could seek to prove his ideas through Scripture, or he could let Scripture speak for itself. He'd been instructed on how to prepare a sermon and how to deliver it once prepared.

But the subject matter that seemed to impact him the most came from the instructors who dealt with the purpose and genuineness of his calling. George Granger, the main organizer of the seminar, had asked the class, "What do you expect to accomplish with your call to preach?"

One young minister had offered, "I want to build a church in an unchurched city. I've been studying the dynamics of church planting and believe I can be successful."

Brother Granger had responded, "Look deeply into your spirit and tell me your primary motivating factor. Is it to be successful as a church planter? Is it so that your friends will recognize you as a success? I'm not asking for a verbal response, but for you to look deeply into your own heart."

Chad had to admit that some of his early visions had been of him standing in front of a large crowd and effectively preaching the gospel. In fact, he was a little bit convicted when Brother Granger went on to say, "Too often, to the young minister, the vision is about himself. The Scripture did say that without a vision the people will perish, but have you ever noticed that it says 'people,' not 'person'?" If the vision is only about you, then only one person will perish. If your vision is truly from God, then it will be about the people."

Then Brother Granger had asked, "Have you ever known a teacher or preacher who seemed to be using the audience for his own advancement rather than really trying to help them? Are you trying to take them somewhere, or are you hoping they will be the means of getting you somewhere?"

Even though Chad was searching his heart for any improper motive, he spoke the appropriate words. "Then I should be more concerned about the conversion and discipling of people than my personal success as a church builder!"

Chad's mind connected Brother Granger's words with those of the elder: "A minister's purpose is like a postman's: deliver the mail faithfully and responsibly. As a pastor I won't be writing the letters; I'll be delivering God's letters. I must not tamper with the message because I am not the Author."

Brother Granger's words gripped him: "As a pastor, you will have to give an account of your actions before Almighty God." It was sobering to know that wherever he went, others would follow. Chad knew that whatever the results, his primary calling was to speak the truth in love. This calling was the most sacred of trusts, so he dared not violate it with personal opinions. Only the truth can set men free. Truth used for any other reason than setting men free is truth misused.

The elder's words were finding an open heart.

Chapter 12

Two Mysteries

*T*he Spirit carries me from The Art Gallery to the ancient city of Jerusalem, where I am to witness a tragic day in the history of the people of Israel. As I arrive, I notice someone else is being escorted to this scene—the prophet Ezekiel—but he is unaware of my presence. God is about to reveal an ominous series of events, the three phases of the departure of His presence from the Temple in Jerusalem.

From the inner court to the threshold

> *Now the cherubims stood on the right side of the house, when the man went in; and the cloud filled the inner court. Then the glory of the LORD went up from the cherub, and stood over the threshold of the house; and the house was filled with the cloud, and the court was full of the brightness of the LORD'S glory. (Ezekiel 10:3–4)*

The glory of Israel has always been her Temple, and the glory of the Temple has always been the presence of God. I have two questions: (1) Why did the Spirit of God leave the place in which He had intended to dwell forever? (See Exodus 15:17; 29:45–46; II Kings 19:15; Psalm 80:1.) The Spirit of God will not remain where it is unwanted, where His law goes unheeded. (2) Why did He leave the Temple and the Holy City in graduated phases instead of all at once? Because God is *longsuffering and gives His people ample opportunity to repent. The anointing does not leave suddenly.*

God seems to be lingering, testing Israel to see if anyone will miss Him after He leaves the inner court. Perhaps someone will cry out for Him to return. How many people will it take to get Him to change His mind? At the time of Abraham's intercession for Sodom, God was willing to spare the entire city if only ten righteous people could be found. It seems, however, that this time the question will go unanswered, for there is not one cry of dismay. No one seems to miss God as He departs from the sanctuary! What a sad day it is when God does not come to church and no one misses Him.

From the threshold to the Eastern Gate

Then the glory of the LORD departed from off the threshold of the house, and stood over the cherubims. And the cherubims lifted up their wings, and mounted up from the earth in my sight: when they went out, the wheels also were beside them, and every one stood at the door of the east gate of the LORD'S house; and the glory of the God of Israel was over them above. (Ezekiel 10:18–19)

God hovers over the threshold of the Temple, possibly hoping someone will notice. If those in the inner court are so cold, surely someone in the outer court will call out to Him. But still, not one seems to miss Him. So He moves from the threshold to the Eastern Gate and pauses to listen. No one cries out. No one misses Him. What a sad state a church can get into!

From the Eastern Gate to the mountain east of the Jerusalem

Then did the cherubims lift up their wings, and the wheels beside them; and the glory of the God of Israel was over them above. And the glory of the LORD went up from the midst of the city, and stood upon the mountain which is on the east side of the city. (Ezekiel 11:22–23)

This time the Spirit of the Lord leaves the Eastern Gate and moves to hover over the mountain east of the city. No one pleads for Him to return, so the glory continues across the mountain until it is out of sight. The house of God has been desolate until this very day. The Spirit takes Ezekiel back to captivity, where he shares his vision.

The Spirit also carries me to another place in time, and I see the Master mourning over the city with a voice full of anguish:

> *O Jerusalem, Jerusalem, the city that kills the prophets and stones those who are sent to it! How often would I have gathered your children together as a hen gathers her brood under her wings, and you were not willing! See, your house is left to you desolate. For I tell you, you will not see me again, until you say, "Blessed is he who comes in the name of the Lord." (Matthew 23:37–39, ESV)*

The glory of the Second Temple

Haggai prophesied that the glory of the Second Temple would exceed the glory of Solomon's Temple (Haggai 2:9). Solomon's Temple had been destroyed in 587 BC when Nebuchadnezzar destroyed Jerusalem and exiled many of the people to Babylon. Seventy years later, when the people returned from Babylon under Ezra, they began building the Second Temple.

When the foundation and the altar of the Temple were completed, the Jews held a great celebration. Oh, what manifestations of joy among the younger generation! "But many of the older priests, Levites, and other leaders who had seen the first Temple, wept aloud when they saw the new Temple's foundation" (Ezra 3:12, NLT). Why were they weeping? Compared to the splendor of Solomon's Temple, the foundation of the Second Temple looked pretty pitiful. Where was the glory Haggai was talking about?

Their question would not be answered until hundreds of years later when God in flesh walked within the walls of the Second Temple. The glory would have dwelt in the Temple if the people would have received Jesus, but they rejected Him: "I am come in my Father's name, and ye receive me not: if another shall come in his own name, him ye will receive." Thus Jesus did not make their house desolate; He left it desolate—in the same state He found it. The Temple and the city that had stood desolate since God's Spirit departed beyond the mountains to the east in Ezekiel's time was still left desolate when they rejected Jesus. But the ultimate desolation is yet to come.

So when you see the abomination of desolation spoken of by the prophet Daniel, standing in the holy place (let the reader understand:). (Matthew 24:15, ESV)

Let no man deceive you by any means: for that day shall not come, except there come a falling away first, and that man of sin be revealed, the son of perdition; who opposeth and exalteth himself above all that is called God, or that is worshipped; so that he as God sitteth in the temple of God, shewing himself that he is God. (II Thessalonians 2:3–4)

The ultimate desolation

The Spirit carries me into the future, and I see the Third Temple, now standing upon the holy mountain. A strange thing has happened. The world leader who at first seemed so wonderful and full of charisma has undergone a personality change. He now stands in the Holy Temple demanding the reverence due only to God. This is the ultimate desolation: Satan, in the form of a man, sitting on the seat ordained for God alone. This progression is a part of the unfolding story of two mysteries, the Mystery of Iniquity and the Mystery of Godliness. This is the ultimate fruit of the two trees.

The two mysteries

I return to The Art Gallery, tasked with portraying the two mysteries on a canvas. But how can I paint such an epic picture on so small a canvas? How can the mysteries of the world be expressed in a few words? Let me trace the journey of the evil mystery. Come with me into my drawing room.

Remember ye not, that, when I was yet with you, I told you these things? And now ye know what withholdeth that he might be revealed in his time. For the mystery of iniquity doth already work: only he who now letteth will let, until he be taken out of the way. And then shall that Wicked be revealed, whom the Lord shall consume with the spirit of his mouth, and shall destroy with the brightness of his coming. (II Thessalonians 2:5–8)

This is the Mystery of Iniquity. It has been brewing since before time began, when there was a rebellion in Heaven.

> *How art thou fallen from heaven, O Lucifer, son of the morning! how art thou cut down to the ground, which didst weaken the nations! For thou hast said in thine heart, I will ascend into heaven, I will exalt my throne above the stars of God: I will sit also upon the mount of the congregation, in the sides of the north: I will ascend above the heights of the clouds; I will be like the most High. Yet thou shalt be brought down to hell, to the sides of the pit. They that see thee shall narrowly look upon thee, and consider thee, saying, Is this the man that made the earth to tremble, that did shake kingdoms; that made the world as a wilderness, and destroyed the cities thereof; that opened not the house of his prisoners? (Isaiah 14:12–17)*

Lucifer began his quest for the throne of God before the world was created and is still continuing his quest through deceptive means. This tool came to be known as the Mystery of Iniquity, and it can be found in the lie Satan told Eve.

"'You will not surely die,' the serpent said to the woman. 'For God knows that when you eat of it your eyes will be opened, and you will be like God, knowing good and evil'" (Genesis 3:4, NIV). Satan's tactic was to hide the Mystery of Iniquity between two distorted truths: you won't die; you will become as gods! Lucifer continues to hide in the Tree of The Knowledge of Good and Evil, and through human philosophy is feeding the same lies to mankind. He appeals to the sovereign nature of man, the image of God. That is why people eat of the fruit; the pride of life is a temptation too strong to ignore.

Satan still uses the same ploy because it works so well. Nimrod was the first man to exalt himself before God. All false religions can be traced back to this concept. Human philosophy always leads to the exaltation of self. The theory of evolution, when carried to its ultimate expression, will claim the deification of man. Every person's rebellion against the law of God lies in this mystery: "I can go my own way. I can determine what is best for me!"

Since man was in the Garden, Satan has been developing the Mystery of Iniquity, priming mankind for his ultimate purpose. When the time is right, he will embody the Antichrist, a bogus imitation of the Mystery of Godliness. The Antichrist will provide the body for

Lucifer's ultimate attempt. He had failed to wrest the throne from the God of Heaven in the beginning; in the end he will wrest away the seat of God on earth. He will sit in the Temple in Jerusalem and declare himself to be God. The Mystery of Iniquity is the ultimate fruit from the other tree. Man will become God—the ultimate abomination, the ultimate lie.

Many people will say, "I'll never go that far!" However, the downward slide is so gradual that it is a mystery how they end up at the bottom so quickly. The poison works slowly, but it can always be traced back to that first time they questioned the Word of God.

There is another mystery, the fruit of the Tree of Life: "And without controversy great is the mystery of godliness: God was manifest in the flesh, justified in the Spirit, seen of angels, preached unto the Gentiles, believed on in the world, received up into glory" (I Timothy 3:16).

This is the Mystery of Godliness: God became man!

It all begin in Genesis 3:15, with the promise of a Messiah, but it has been the plan of God since the foundation of the world. On Mount Moriah Abraham prophesied, "God will provide himself a lamb." He turned and saw a ram caught in the thicket. At Calvary God did provide Himself as a Lamb, slain from the foundation of the world. John the Baptist proclaimed, "Behold, the Lamb of God that takes away the sins of the world!" (See John 1:29.) Isaiah prophesied, "They shall call His name Emmanuel, which being interpreted is, God is with us" (Matthew 1:23; c.f. Isaiah 7:14). But the Mystery of Godliness began thousands of years before that.

> *In the beginning was the Word*
> *The Word was with God*
> *The Word was God*
> *And the Word was made flesh!*

There are two trees with two resulting mysteries. The Mystery of Iniquity claims that man will become god. The Mystery of Godliness declares that God became man. The Mystery of Iniquity has its seeds in the Tree of the Knowledge of Good and Evil. The Mystery of Godliness is the Tree of Life, the Living Word Incarnate.

Which mystery guides your life? Do you trust in human reasoning? Have you swallowed the lie of Satan, the author of the Mystery of

Iniquity? Or do you still hold to the precious hope of God in Christ, reconciling the world unto Himself?

Remember Satan wants you to believe you can become a god; God wants you to believe that He became a man. One is the fruit called logic; the other is the fruit called Logos. One is abstract; the other is concrete. One is mythology; the other is history (His story). I choose to believe His story. After all, I have been to the Garden of God. I am a concrete man in an abstract world.

ॐ

Spring break was over, and Chad returned to the seminary invigorated with the lively discussions and spiritual atmosphere he had experienced at the seminar for young ministers. Therefore, entering the Religious Philosophy classroom on Monday morning was like being slapped in the face with a wet blanket. There was Professor Clark, pushing his glasses to the bridge of his nose, clearing his throat, tamping his notes on the podium. There were Chad's friends, looking at him, wondering why he would rather spend spring break at a church function than have a good time with his friends. There were his other classmates, buzzing with tales of all the fun they'd enjoyed. He felt as bewildered and alone as an ugly duckling among the swans. He really didn't belong here.

As usual, Professor Clark had written the topic of the day on the whiteboard: "Doxastic Voluntarism." He rapped for order and said, "If you've done the required reading over spring break, you should be able to define today's topic." Chad hadn't had time to study the material in depth that week, but he had looked it over the night before.

Clark called on someone, who was obviously unprepared. "Um, doxasystic volun . . . um . . ."

Clark frowned. "Come on, people. Has anyone cracked the dictionary of philosophical terms required for this class? Today's topic is pronounced 'dox·ast'·ic vol·un·tār·ism.' Now who did the reading? Who can define the term?"

John raised his hand and the professor acknowledged him, saying, "OK, Foster. Put it in the simplest terms possible."

John said, "Doxastic voluntarism is when people choose their own beliefs. Like, they have a certain amount of control over what they believe."

Nicole said, "I got the idea from the reading that people don't cause themselves to believe something, but their beliefs simply form over time."

The professor nodded. "OK, let's go a step further. Who can explain the difference between direct doxastic voluntarism and indirect doxastic voluntarism?" He acknowledged another student, who said, "Well, the meanings are so close it's hard to make a distinction, but I'd say direct doxastic voluntarism is when people have *direct voluntary control* over at least some of their beliefs, like, for example, they could change their belief from theism to atheism. Indirect doxastic voluntarism is when people have *unintended voluntary control* over at least some of their beliefs through voluntary intermediate actions, like, for example, by doing research and evaluating the evidence."

Clark asked, "How then would you define doxastic *in*voluntarism?" No one raised a hand. "Anyone? No? Well, an example of doxastic involuntarism would be that people are unable to choose what they believe; their beliefs are imposed upon them. We can see this most clearly by comparing the religions of different cultures. We do not decide which faith to believe in, we are born into that faith with parents. Even those who convert are converting because their needs are better met and their intellectual abilities are better suited over one faith for another so they are drawn to that new faith."

He continued, "So if I could acquire a belief at will, presumably I could decide to acquire it whether or not it was true. If, in full consciousness, I could will to acquire a 'belief' irrespective of its truth, it is unclear that before the event I could seriously think of it as a 'belief'; instead, it would be something purporting to represent reality. But who would accept a belief when one already has the understanding of its truth or not? It would no longer be a 'belief' as we understand the term but an 'understanding.' Therefore, beliefs are actually accepted without investigation and are not sought out but forced upon us."

The students sat like wooden Indians looking at Professor Clark with blank stares. Was the professor deliberately trying to cloud every religious issue? Was he deliberately trying to destroy everyone's belief system?

Without waiting for further comments, Clark continued, "Remember we've discussed that thinking critically about religious beliefs might indicate they are flawed in a number of ways: inconsistent, contradictory, without evidence to support the basic claims. But this doesn't mean that philosophy attempts to disprove religious beliefs. Philosophy has come to reveal that religious beliefs are just that—beliefs and not empirical claims. Philosophy helps us to understand this."

Dan whispered under his breath, "Thanks for clearing that up."

Chad's brain was awhirl like gears in a clock, clicking, turning, meshing, leading to nowhere. He had gotten to the place where he dreaded coming to class. Whatever happened to a simple biblical belief system?

Chad turned to the inside front cover of his notebook and read again the words he'd written in bold letters at the beginning of the semester: "Beware lest any man spoil you through philosophy and vain deceit, after the tradition of men, after the rudiments of the world, and not after Christ" (Colossians 1:8). Now he added another passage: "Faith is the substance of things hoped for, the evidence of things not seen . . . Through faith we understand that the worlds were framed by the word of God, so that things which are seen were not made of things which do appear" (Hebrews 11:1, 3).

Professor Clark had said beliefs are not empirical claims. But God's Word said faith is the *substance* of things that *can't be seen*. Those unseen things were more real than the things that *could* be seen. Chad thought of the elder's words: "Beware, young preacher, for the time will come when the very book they teach, the Holy Bible, will no longer be considered the absolute Word of God. 'Inerrant' will become 'inspired,' and from there it is but a slippery slope."

It gave him comfort to know he was not the first one to do battle with the intrusion of human philosophy into the realm of religion. He couldn't wait until school was out that day so he could revisit The Art Gallery. He'd seen the title of chapter 13 in the elder's manuscript: "Strong Delusion." That sounded a little ominous, but anything was better than the hour he had just endured.

Strong Delusion

*E*veryone wanders into The Art Gallery at some point in time, but, as the Curator will tell you, many don't stay long enough to discover the deeper truths in the back room. In fact, many never make it past the strange abstract painting that always seems to be displayed in the most conspicuous place.

Why is the abstract painting allowed in the gallery? Why did God place the Tree of The Knowledge of Good and Evil in the Garden of Eden? Why does God send a strong delusion? Because the sovereign mind of man must have an avenue of expression and choice, even if that avenue leads to his own destruction.

I stand again in The Art Gallery, gazing at the abstract painting. My concrete mind asks a question that puzzles me: "Why would anyone want to enter the abstract?"

Helen Wyner was a dedicated young lady, one who had proven faithful to the church during her teen years. Her pastor and youth minister spoke well of her, and the general congregation often remarked on her spiritual zeal and maturity.

Yet like all teens, Helen struggled with her self-image. Though she was an attractive girl, she wondered if there ever would be a special man in her life. Many young men had shown interest, but for various reasons the relationships had never become serious. This trend continued throughout high school and college.

At the risk of being labeled a pessimist, I must state that dreams do not always come to pass—and when they do, there are always *alterations in the details. "Tall, dark, and handsome" may come to life as "short, pale, and whatever." After all, beauty is in the eye of the beholder.*

Helen had emotional moments as she faced the possibility that things might not turn out as she wanted. Still, she clung tenaciously to her vision of a perfect mate sharing her life.

Then that vision began to take form in a young coworker, Brian Wesley. But there was one problem: Brian was not a Christian. The concrete says, "What fellowship has light with darkness?" Concrete does not make exceptions.

One day Helen was wandering through The Art Gallery and came across the abstract painting. She gazed into its alluring message and was spellbound by its logic that seemed to say, "Brian seems like such a nice young man. Perhaps you can win him. What could go wrong on one date? God will understand." Abstract is always an expert on what God understands. To learn what God really understands, one must read His book.

Strong delusion insinuated itself into Helen's thinking. Truth said, "Don't search for love; search for life and let love find you." Delusion said, "One short detour from the concrete won't harm you."

Helen's friends began noticing a change in her focus. The one who had volunteered for every ministry began avoiding their fellowship, and her spiritual sensitivity began to wane. Her trips to The Art Gallery became more frequent, but she always ended up standing in front of the abstract painting of strong delusion, the one that appears however a person wants it to appear. Truth would have given her absolute laws to ponder, but abstract was showing her what her wandering heart desired to see. She made too many trips, too many philosophical wanderings. One day the lure was so strong that she entered the abstract.

Justin Marston had been blessed with a marvelous mind, a fact that was obvious to everyone around him. His schoolteachers and Christian educators were impressed at how quickly he grasped new ideas and facts. The teachers frequently found themselves asking the class, "Does anyone besides Justin know the answer?"

Along with Justin's great mental faculties came a true compassion—a passion to help his fellow man. He was moved by the needs of others and felt a call of God to minister to them, maybe not a pulpit ministry, but a definite call to care and counseling.

There is a vicious war raging between the concepts of biblical counseling and those of human philosophy. There is certainly room for reasoning within the Word of God, but the battle boldly rages to push the mind of the student outside the parameters of God's Word. Many have slipped on the treacherous slopes of therapy and counseling. As an elder, it's not my purpose to decry the profession, but I must issue a strong warning. Human psychology is founded in the abstract, and the seeds of its fruit have their origin in the Tree of the Knowledge of Good and Evil.

Sadly, a constant diet of education in human philosophy began to erode Justin's confidence in the absoluteness of God's Word. He received his education in The Art Gallery, but made few trips to the beautiful portrayal of the Garden of God. In fact, he seemed to be aware of only one painting—the abstract.

The words of his pastor no longer had the same effect. While there certainly was a place for Christian guidance counseling, he instead found himself questioning basic truths that he should have settled in his mind long before, that he thought he had already settled. Logic began to sit in judgment over Logos.

Justin began missing church. After all, he had a hectic schedule, and once again he thought God would understand.

The skilled instructor stood before the abstract painting. It was a red-letter day for education. He made it seem so inviting. The pure Word was no longer illuminating Justin's path; instead, strong delusion was making a big play for his mind. The prime young man with the brilliant mind finally made his decision and followed his guide into the abstract.

George and Pat Gordon seemed to be model Christians. They were faithful in every definition of the word, the kind of couple a pastor dreams of having in his congregation.

When Catherine was born, they couldn't wait to bring her to the altar in her little white dress and have their beloved pastor pray the prayer of dedication. They felt the same way when Roger and Annie joined the family.

By this time, the Gordons had accepted the position of youth ministers, and they diligently taught the concrete Word of God to the precious teens of Cornerstone Church. The pastor didn't worry about the training his youth were receiving, for George and Pat were dedicated and diligent.

But the time came when Catherine, Roger, and Annie were old enough to join the youth group. Sadly, the greatest trap often occurs when parents begin teaching their own children. Were they willing to take the same stand with their own children that they for years had asked other parents to take? It is one thing to have a good philosophy on child-rearing and quite another thing to actually apply it. Many great leaders have failed this test and lost respect because of their error.

When Catherine began asking questions about the family rules and church standards, it became increasingly challenging to give an answer. Roger complained that his school friends could do things he wasn't allowed to do, and they all were churchgoers. Annie had an issue with the way she was supposed to dress. She often cried because she looked different from all the other girls in her school classroom. The Gordons discovered that teaching once a week was easier than answering these questions on a daily basis. Being honest parents, they made many trips to The Art Gallery to discover the true answers to their children's questions.

They gazed quite often at the infamous abstract painting. In fact, they began to listen to it more than to their once-beloved pastor. Abstract philosophy began showing up in their teaching, and they eventually found themselves in conference with the pastor. In previous times they were able to give answers, but this time all they had were questions. Concrete gives answers; abstract asks questions.

They finally found a beach-house church across town that could give them what they wanted, and their kids could be like all the other kids at school. One fateful day they entered The Art Gallery, bypassed the beautiful rendition of the Garden of God, and walked boldly into the abstract.

Bob Spacer couldn't remember when he was not called to preach. If anyone asked, he would say he was born to preach. When he was younger, and everyone called him Bobby, he would set up a little pulpit in the living room and rehearse last Sunday's sermon for the family. It was a foregone conclusion that he was destined for the pulpit.

When he was thirteen, he preached his first youth service. He fasted for three days and prayed for hours for this fifteen-minute "masterpiece." The Spirit moved and the youth group responded to the message with intense prayer. Bobby was on his way.

He received a scholarship to seminary and spent four years at the feet of scholars of the Word. He then marched out onto the evangelistic field to challenge churches throughout North America.

During his first seven years as an evangelist, he had a reputation for preaching the pure Word of God without compromise. He and his wife were the epitome of godliness.

Then the call came for him to pastor a progressive church in a mid-size city. It was a church with a lot of growth potential. Bob tackled this latest challenge with the same zeal and passion he had always possessed. He soon had a flock of new converts to add to his already thriving church.

But the questions began to fly. "Why does pastor so-and-so allow this, but you preach against it?" "Why can't the youth group do this? Others allow it!"

It seems that holding the line is always a battle, for the tendency of human nature is to "kick against the pricks." The best pastors sometimes become weary in the battle. Instead of taking the time for spiritual refreshing, pastors like Bob keep steady at the grind, and they often wear down.

To Bob, the abstract began to appear less stressful than the concrete. On his latest visit to The Art Gallery, he stared into the abstract painting. In direct disobedience to the Word, he had become weary in well doing. A gospel that didn't call for commitment seemed more attractive. After all, everyone must be saved by grace. Maybe he should just preach grace and ignore righteousness and true holiness.

Jesus can justify the sinner, but He never justifies the sin. Bob's preaching began to sound abstract. Ephesians 2:8–9 became his go-to passage, with verse 10 conveniently left out. He failed to mention that although salvation doesn't come by works, salvation does result in works, which had been God's plan from the very beginning.

Some of his friends had already entered the abstract, and they made it sound so inviting. He found himself looking into it more and more. It seemed like an easier way. (It is really a harder way.)

Finally, he stood in the pulpit and made it official. He would no longer take the stands he had taken before. Bob entered the world of the abstract.

The case of Mel Langston is perhaps the most tragic of all. Mel was a new babe in Christ with a zeal and hunger for God. He was willing to be taught, but had the misfortune of "praying through" in a church in which no one had the time to teach Bible studies. The law of spiritual evolution was in force—survival of the fittest. Few new converts can survive in this atmosphere.

Make no mistake. His pastor made up for his lack of time invested in new converts by a weekly blast of spiritual arctic air from the pulpit. His ferocious diatribes on separation from sin left no doubt as to where he stood. His bold proclamations went forth from a love-starved heart and landed with the solid thud of legalism. Men of this nature scar the face of true holiness more than their abstract counterparts. Truth was never meant to be a club with which to wound God's children.

Mel tried to obey everything he heard preached, but no one ever sat down with him and taught him these principles from the Bible in a more conducive atmosphere. Devoid of a true love relationship with Jesus Christ, Mel began to desire something more than he had received. Because he did not have a solid foundation in truth, he was a prime candidate for recruit by abstract forces. As he wandered through The Art Gallery, he was drawn to the colorful abstract painting. One sad day he entered it. What a sad thing it is when those who hold truth cannot match their love for truth with a love for people. We must speak the truth in love.

What is your story? Have I come close to telling it? Have you been making trips to The Art Gallery and gazing into the abstract? If so, please remember that many who enter it will not return.

I go daily to the museum and always stop and gaze at the abstract. Not that I am tempted to enter, for I have seen reality and have made my decision. I simply want to be here should someone ever return from behind the canvas, someone with their belly full of empty promises and pitiful mirages. I have had some success.

Helen returned one day, and I was there waiting for her. Brian wasn't with her, but she brought little Heather. We love little Heather. In fact, I have been to court several times to testify in custody battles. Heather is learning about God, but every other weekend she is with her dad and she always comes home with a lot of questions. We believe the truth will win out, but Helen must pray daily for God's help. She carries reminders of her journey into the abstract.

Justin came back from behind the canvas one day, and then disappeared behind it the next. He came back to me the next day, and then left the following day. He really longs for the simple faith of his youth, but I wonder if he will ever recover from the philosophical poison that corrupted his brilliant mind.

I have never heard from George and Pat, and Bob seems to have disappeared, but I come daily to the museum and stand before the painting, hoping against hope they will return. As for Mel, it is my prayer that one day he will realize that love and truth can exist together and then he will find someone to heal the wounds inflicted by a "lord over God's heritage."

I cannot—must not—go behind the canvas except to seek for my friends. Most of all, I can make certain that someone is here for them should they ever return. I know my calling. I am a concrete man in an abstract world.

ớ∞ó

Chad was especially preoccupied when he made his way into The Art Gallery on Friday, the week after spring break. But he was jolted from his thoughts when he saw that John Foster had entered the gallery ahead of him. As far as he knew, John had never come to the gallery on his own, and the one time he had come with Chad, he had vowed never to come again. So what was his friend doing here?

Unnoticed, Chad held back, hoping against hope that John had had a change of heart. He would be overjoyed if John was searching for a deeper relationship with God. Thus he was horrified when John entered the room where the infamous abstract painting was displayed.

John stood in rapt attention, gazing at the abstract with its thick layers of paint that projected a three-dimensional image. Its garish colors and odd shapes captured his imagination like nothing had before. Ever since the day he had come here with his friends, this painting had dominated his thinking. Something about it was irresistible, and he felt compelled to return to The Art Gallery to study it one more time.

It had been a long time since John had knelt before God in diligent prayer. He had become absorbed in his own thoughts and reasoning, and this path was much more appealing to his spiritually deprived mind. The innocence of his childhood faith had given way to a quagmire of human ideas and religious concepts. He was a searcher, no doubt, but he was unaware that his search had led him down the wrong path.

That path of error had led him to delusion, and now he stood teetering on the edge, about to leap into the abstract that to him seemed so new and exciting. He felt a strong pull and surrendered himself to it . . .

Transfixed, Chad watched John for several minutes, hoping for the best. What would his friend do? His heartrate suddenly quickened as he sensed the moment of crisis. Something seemed to rip his heart apart as he saw his lifelong friend slip behind the canvas.

Chad screamed out, "Wait, John! Don't go there!" But the words just echoed through the gallery. It was too late. His wayward friend had disappeared behind the canvas. With a broken heart, Chad acknowledged to himself that those who make that leap seldom return.

Oh, the anguish of spirit! What were the words Paul used to describe it in reference to Christ? "He suffered such contradiction." That's what Chad was feeling—contradiction. But how could sorrow and joy cohabitate? Joy comes when you have seen the truth, but sorrow intrudes because others have been blinded to it. Elation is the result of knowing you have discovered the right path, but heartbreak happens because a loved one has been swallowed up in the abstract.

That was the correct word for it—love. Love is the most beautiful feeling in the world, but it also can lead to one of the most painful experiences one will ever know. This was another ministry lesson for the young preacher. People cannot love without making themselves vulnerable. Love rips out the defense mechanism. The same love that drives a minister to reach for someone opens the door for that person to wound him. "He was wounded for our transgressions." He was vulnerable. No one had ever left himself more vulnerable than Jesus Christ. The enemy dealt Him a terrible wound while His arms were outstretched in a defenseless position.

For an instant, Chad felt the pain of crucifixion. Then John 3:16 came to mind, and he felt the power of resurrection. One cannot really read that verse; he must feel it. *God so loved . . .* There was a groan in that love. God so loved that He gave . . .

That was it! Love gives, but it is not always reciprocated. Did not Paul say that he would gladly spend and be spent for the people, but it seemed that the more he loved the less he was loved?

Chad knew there were those who loved true ministers of God. He certainly loved Pastor Hanson, a man who did not have the level of education Chad had achieved, but a man who loved God and truth, who was wise in years and experience, and who took to heart the call of ministry. Pastor Hanson would be brokenhearted when he heard about John. The elder of The Art Gallery had expressed the same sorrow in his parchment because some of his friends also had disappeared behind the abstract canvas.

Chad's dilemma was what to do next. He couldn't pretend like nothing had happened. He could never forget John and their shared backgrounds and good times together. He was pondering this when he recalled God's admonition to the prophet Samuel. He realized Samuel had felt the same contradiction as he mourned over the failure of Saul. God's words had jolted Samuel from his lamentation: "Fill your horn with oil and go!" Chad's spirit quickened. Somewhere a David was waiting to be anointed.

What could Chad do? The answer was simple. He must pursue his calling and reach for those whose hearts were open. At the same time, he would make it a personal priority to be there should John or any of his other friends emerge from error.

With that settled, he turned another page in the elder's manuscript.

Chapter 14

Sailing the Sea

As a concrete man, I cannot live defensively in an abstract world; I do not merely "hold the fort," as the saying goes. The kingdom of God must advance, so the concrete must invade the abstract. Therefore, it becomes necessary for the visionary to launch out into the abstract sea.

In creation, God called the concrete out of the abstract. In regeneration, God calls the concrete out of the abstract. Just as the earth was without form and void until God moved on the face of the waters, so is the lost soul drowning in the abstract until something concrete is formed within him. If the lost will be rescued from the waters of chaos, someone must be bold enough to go sailing on the sea.

Lighthouses are safe havens from the storms of life, but they are not built to house great crowds of people. Soldiers of the Word do not cower in the corners of lighthouses waiting for deliverance from above; they get out of the boat and walk on water!

The concrete is known to produce men of vision such as Peter, who dared to go into the danger zone. These visionaries venture out upon the abstract, knowing that only the miracle power of God will keep them from sinking beneath the surface. They walk on water, and if they dare take their eyes off Jesus they begin to sink. Will you venture into the realm where only the power of God will preserve you? If so, you can be a guide to souls drowning in the abstract. You can bring them back into the lighthouse.

God looked down and observed a world that had gone astray. The waters of the abstract, the fruit of the Tree of the Knowledge of Good and Evil, were increasing each day. As the waters crept higher, the solid concrete law of God seemed to recede. Every day brought more abstract and less concrete. Man was absorbed with himself, seeking to gratify himself, pursuing the Mystery of Iniquity.

> *And it came to pass, when men began to multiply on the face of the earth, and daughters were born unto them, that the sons of God saw the daughters of men that they were fair; and they took them wives of all which they chose. And the LORD said, My spirit shall not always strive with man, for that he also is flesh: yet his days shall be an hundred and twenty years. There were giants in the earth in those days; and also after that, when the sons of God came in unto the daughters of men, and they bare children to them, the same became mighty men which were of old, men of renown. And GOD saw that the wickedness of man was great in the earth, and that every imagination of the thoughts of his heart was only evil continually. And it repented the LORD that he had made man on the earth, and it grieved him at his heart. (Genesis 6:1–6)*

Man's every thought was evil. Any semblance of pursuing God had been abandoned. Every individual was seeking his or her own way. The waters of the abstract were rising at an alarming rate. How could such a world survive? When the waters of the abstract got high enough, all of humanity drowned in the flood. Only one kind of man could survive the flood, a concrete man like Noah. In his day, he was the only concrete man in an abstract world.

If the world wanted abstract, God would give them abstract. They liked the instability of water, so that's what they got. The greatest fear of the sinner should be that God will turn him over to his own desires. When God becomes vexed and grants every corrupt wish, death is imminent. Why should He destroy man when He can simply let man destroy himself?

God brought land out of water. God brought the concrete out of the abstract. There was no life on earth until the concrete was formed. Out of earth came more life. The thriving vegetation was a testimony to the fruitfulness of the concrete. Why should the earth desire to return to its void state? Why should man desire the abstract in which nothing can permanently survive?

God rescued me from the abstract world of human philosophy and planted my feet on a solid foundation. Where death once reigned, now there is life. I have no desire to return to the abstract. It would be much like a dog returning to its own vomit or a sow, once washed clean, returning to wallow in the mire. (See II Peter 2:22.) Yet that is exactly what mankind did.

Their only hope was one concrete man named Noah who was sailing through an abstract world. It is possible to sail upon the abstract, but it is not easy. Noah possessed two necessary qualities: the character of the sailor and the construction of the vessel.

The Character of the Sailor

"These are the generations of Noah: Noah was a just man and perfect in his generations, and Noah walked with God" (Genesis 6:9). No other aspect is as important in a leader as good character. (See II Peter 1:5–8.) If a person does not have good character, leadership will destroy him. A rocking vessel on a storm-tossed sea will reveal a person's true nature. Things hidden in the normal flow of life become boldly exposed once the mantle of leadership is bestowed.

"Some men's sins are open beforehand, going before to judgment; and some men they follow after. Likewise also the good works of some are manifest beforehand; and they that are otherwise cannot be hid" (I Timothy 5:24–25). This biblical passage has to do with leadership. Some men's sins and faults are so obvious beforehand that we show wisdom in not anointing them for leadership. However, some men's sins are hidden until after the mantle has fallen upon them. All progressive pastors have certainly experienced this calamity. Some people are successful in a supporting role, but when promoted to leadership they are destroyed. There is both great danger and great reward to the man that sails upon the sea!

Noah was a just man. This means he was:

(1) Righteous in government
(2) Right in his cause
(3) Righteous in conduct and character
(4) Righteous as justified and vindicated by God.

Noah did not have ulterior motives. He exercised righteous government, his cause was legitimate, he conducted himself in a righteous manner, and he was right in the eyes of God.

Noah was "perfect" in his generations, meaning he was complete, whole, and entire. He pursued everything God had for him. He was not a casual believer, but one who sought to do everything that pleased God and to avoid everything that displeased the Lord.

Noah walked with God, not for Him but with Him. The leader must get beyond doing things for God and begin doing things with God. When Peter took his eyes off of Jesus, he could not walk on the water. One can only walk on the abstract with God; one cannot walk on the abstract for God. This requires relationship, which is an ongoing thing. One can know another person without seeing him frequently, but one must interact consistently to have a true relationship. Sailor, be warned: do not venture out upon the abstract seas without a good relationship with Jesus Christ!

The character of the sailor is crucial to the success of the enterprise. A sailor with poor character will be swallowed up by the abstract. Instead of returning to the lighthouse, he will venture into the beach house. He can't simply believe a few concrete principles; he must be a concrete man.

The Construction of the Vessel

Not only must the sailor have good character, he must have a strong vessel. The waves of the abstract will beat heavily upon the craft, and it will not survive unless it is constructed according to God's plan.

Noah had never seen rain. He had no experience building a boat. There were no manuals to consult, no experts to go to for guidance. There was no room for trial and error. I am certain there were some ingenious boatbuilders in Noah's day, but only one boat was sturdy enough to survive the violent onslaught of abstract waters. This was the boat that Noah built, and there was only one place to go to get advice for building this kind of vessel.

God gave specific instructions:

Make thee an ark of gopher wood; rooms shalt thou make in the ark, and shalt pitch it within and without with pitch. And this is the fashion which thou shalt make it of: The length of the ark shall be three hundred cubits, the breadth of it fifty cubits, and the height of it thirty cubits. A window shalt thou make to the ark, and in a cubit shalt thou finish it above; and the door of the ark shalt thou set in the side thereof; with lower, second, and third stories shalt thou make it. (Genesis 6:14–16)

We see in Genesis 6:22 that Noah followed these instructions explicitly: "Thus did Noah; according to all that God commanded him, so did he."

The Word of God is concrete. The Word of God is the Tree of Life. The Word of God is settled. Though all else is swallowed up in the abstract sea, the Word of God will never pass away. Build your boat according to the book. It takes a concrete vessel to float in abstract waters.

If you are determined to sail the sea, I bid you a safe journey. Remember to search for lighthouses along the way; avoid the beach houses. Don't stay gone too long, but return to the concrete as often as possible. Don't be lured by the soft waves of the abstract or fooled when the south wind blows softly. Remember no man can stay above the abstract unless Jesus Christ is with him. Never trust the abstract. Be a concrete man in an abstract world.

ॐ

Chad was back on familiar turf. How many hours had he spent in the home of his beloved pastor? The time had come to sit down with his mentor and share with him the details of his recent journey. The elder's allegory about sailing the sea had branded into the young man's soul just how treacherous the ministry can become. It was a little overwhelming to contemplate the concrete sailing on the abstract!

The elder's words about the character of the sailor hit home. To Chad, that is what stood out about Pastor Hanson. He did not promote himself but taught that promotion comes from the Lord. Chad could not think of one thing his mentor preached that he himself did not live out. Chad asked himself, "What is greater? The sermon I preach with my mouth, or the sermon I preach with my life?" That line of thought had brought him to the pastor's home.

Chad's first question for Pastor Hanson was, "Did you ever find yourself in a place where you were tempted to bend the rules a little, if you know what I mean? From my perspective, it seems that you have always held a steady line, but I'm starting to see that each person has his own battles to fight."

The wise pastor replied, "Each man has his journey, and if he is sincere, there will be moments of questioning. If I were to say it is dangerous to be sincere, what would it mean to you?"

"It would mean that a person with a sincere heart will be tested in his faith," said Chad. "This test is inevitable. If one prefers comfort and compromise, sincerity can be dangerous to him because he won't pass the test."

"That's correct. So, to answer your question directly, I have certainly had my moments of conflict. Sometimes the greatest battles involve those to whom you are closest. Such is the dilemma of wearing the two hats of father and pastor. It is not easy to wear those hats at the same time on the same head."

Chad was a little surprised at this. "But you have such a beautiful family. I can't imagine there ever being moments of conflict."

"So you say," the pastor said with a smile. "Someday you will see that life presents no perfect scenarios. I do have an awesome family that has stood with me through thick and thin. But I have watched my own children go through the battles of submission and dedication to God. They have to make their own sacrifices and receive their own calling. I remember one time asking God why my sacrifice wasn't good enough for my children. But that's not the way it works. A father's heart wants to make it easier for them, but a pastor's heart knows they must pay the price for their own ministry. It is tough when both hearts beat in the same chest. Oh, the wisdom in our Lord's statement, 'Blessed is he who is not offended in Me.'"

Chad was surprised at the direction the conversation had taken. "But you did make the correct call!"

His mentor said, "I certainly hope so. I just had to remind myself that they were God's children before they were mine." He then shared another experience. "I once asked God what message He wanted me to preach to the children and young people of the church. I needed to know how strong of a stand I should take. God answered me very simply by asking me what I wanted my own children to believe. I had no problem answering that one. I wanted my children to believe the absolute truth of God's Word and be founded upon true Christian principles. God then told me, 'If it's good enough for your children, then it's good enough for everyone else's children.'"

"How did you make it through those challenging times?" asked Chad.

"I'll give you three answers," replied Pastor Hanson. "First, you must always maintain a strong relationship with God. A prayerless preacher will not remain faithful to truth. Second, fall in love with the Word of God. By that I mean don't just look at it as a sermon resource; see it as a book to live by. Read it daily for devotion and do your sermon preparation at another time. And third, open your life to mentors, elders whom you have given the right to speak into your life at any time, leaders to whom you are accountable. If you silence the voices of mentors, you will most certainly fall."

Tears formed in Chad's eyes. "Pastor, I have to admit that I was on a slippery slope for a while."

"I know. I've been watching you."

"I visited The Art Gallery and found the old manuscript of the elder. I think I mentioned it to you."

A smile creased Hanson's face. "Ah, The Art Gallery. And what did you learn?'

"I learned that the truth upon which I was established is indeed the truth. For that, I must thank you."

They both sat in silence for a while, then Pastor Hanson said, "I'm so proud of you and the journey you have made. It is my dream that you will fly higher than I have ever flown. Each generation is the foundation off of which the next generation launches. Sail on, my son! But remember that he who sails on the sea of life must have an anchor. You must have accountability in your life."

Chad bowed his head and replied, "I'm ready."

"Son, I have known all along that you have good character; just as I knew that John was wrestling with troubling thoughts. Each man must follow the course God has set for him, but I want to set some parameters for you to assure that you stay on course."

He then handed Chad a document detailing the following points of accountability:

Make Time Each Week for These Questions

(1) How has God blessed you this week? What went right?

(2) What problem or concern has consumed your thoughts this week? What went wrong?

(3) What has God shown you from His Word this week? Beware of the Bible becoming only a source for sermons.

Questions pertaining to spiritual life:

(1) Describe your prayer life (for yourself, others, praise, confession, gratitude)
(2) How is your relationship with Christ changing?
(3) How have you been tempted this week? In what ways? How did you respond?
(4) Do you have any unconfessed sin in your life?
(5) Are you walking in the Spirit? What spiritual encounters have you had?

Questions Pertaining to Home Life

(1) How is your relationship with your wife? Love is spelled T-I-M-E. Do you make time (date night or lunch) to talk with her and encourage the sharing of her feelings and concerns without letting the church dominate every conversation?
(2) Do you let her know (words, gifts, helps, etc.) she is still the most special person in your life?
(3) How is your relationship with your children? Are you spending quality time with them according to their ages and needs? Are you fun to live with? Are you intentionally teaching them values, discipline, and character? How effective are you in their spiritual training?
(4) How are your finances? (e.g., stewardship, management, goals, give some, save some, spend some.) This often is an area of struggle for a young family and church-planter.

Question Pertaining to Work Life

(1) How are things on your job: relationships, temptations, progress, stress, problems?

Critical Concerns

(1) Do you feel in the center of God's will? Do you sense His peace?
(2) What are you wrestling with in your thought life?
(3) What have you done for someone else this week?
(4) Are your priorities in the right order?
(5) Is your moral and ethical behavior what it should be?
(6) How are you doing in your personal high-risk area?
(7) Are the "visible you" and "the real you" consistent in this relationship?

The list of accountabilities did not make Chad feel violated or threatened; instead, it gave him a sense of security. Seeing John disappear into the abstract, seeing Dan Wilkins and Jerry Dotson get sand in their eyes, and seeing Lisa just disappear into anywhere, made him realize how dangerous an undisciplined life can become.

He left Pastor Hanson's home with a promise—or better yet, a covenant—that he would always leave the door open for a voice of guidance in his life. He knew now that this entire journey had been his spiritual graduation.

Just a few more trips to The Art Gallery, and he would be on his way.

Chapter 15

Right to the Tree of Life

I return again to The Art Gallery, but my spirit tells me I am *nearing the end of my journey. But I must make one more visit into the painting of the Garden of God. I did not know that I would return, but I must.*

My soul takes me into the Garden of God.

The peaceful bliss I find here is like a dewy morning, unsullied by the wrongs of mankind. Can you imagine living in a world without sin, without malice, without ulterior motive, and without the heaviness of carnal knowledge? Do you know some things you would like to forget? Are there ideas and memories etched into your mind that hound you? Does human philosophy constantly attempt to force itself into your thoughts?

The beautiful atmosphere in Eden is free of these fruits of evil. The spirit of truth is so pure that I am tempted to believe I could live forever without natural nourishment. Adam and Eve in Paradise— what could possibly tempt them to give it all up? Mankind has already walked down this beaten path; we know the ploy of Satan in his temptation of man. We know why mankind fell. My purpose for this visit is quite different. I want to know how man can return to Paradise. Is there a key to the restoration of the soul?

"There is no fear in love; but perfect love casteth out fear: because fear hath torment. He that feareth is not made perfect in love" (I John 4:18). The trust a child has in his parents is akin to the trust I should have in God. Why should I doubt someone who loves me completely? If I know His love for me is perfect, then I trust He will never allow

anything to happen to me that will harm me. In fact, He will see that all things work together for my good. This is life in the Garden of God—no worries, no fears. Just total trust in God.

The formula for peace can be found in God's Word. Revelation 20 tells us of the time coming when there will be a thousand years of peace on earth. What brings this peace? First, Satan will be bound. Second, Jesus Christ will reign.

Before Satan entered the Garden of God there was only the simple reign of God. The absence of the enemy and presence of God brings peace. Oh, that man could return to those days!

But wait a minute! Some will return to the Tree of Life. Some will find this peace: "Blessed are they that do his commandments, that they may have right to the tree of life, and may enter in through the gates into the city" (Revelation 22:14).

Could it be as simple as obedience? If all sin is disobedience, then the solution must be obedience. Perhaps the battle for the restoration of the soul begins and ends in simple obedience to God's Word, the Logos, the fruit of the Tree of Life.

I return to The Art Gallery and continue my quest for restoration. I have seen the way man lived when he lived in innocence. Now I want to see how man lives when he is allowed to follow his own conscience.

My spirit takes me on a stroll with a man named Enoch, the seventh from Adam through Seth, the righteous seed. Seven is God's number of completion or perfection. There is another seventh from Adam through Cain—a reprobate named Lamech. Lamech symbolizes the complete picture of those that eat the fruit of the Tree of the Knowledge of Good and Evil. The end result is a seared conscience that is callous to the point that it cannot comprehend the righteousness of God. This is the atmosphere of the world in which Enoch lived.

Enoch and I are walking together, but there's also a third party; Enoch walks with God. That is really all I know—the Bible does not provide any details. I am the silent observer as Enoch and his God stroll along, conversing. They speak like old friends, and I get the idea there's nothing they wouldn't do for each other. Today they seem to be especially close. I watch them, but I cannot hear what they are saying. Whatever it is, it is special, and this particular stroll is special. So special that Enoch never returns. Somewhere over a rise or around a bend, I lose sight of them. They have disappeared, for God took Enoch home with Him.

One man let his conscience lead him to God. One man became a type for us all. The seventh from Adam, of the righteous seed, was caught away from this earth. This was a preview of the day when the righteous children of God will be caught up from this earth. God is trying to tell man that obedience to His law is the way to life.

We have seen how mankind lived in innocence, and we have observed what happened when human conscience took over. What happens when mankind is under his own government?

When mankind was released to govern himself, the fallen human spirit took over. Nimrod appeared on the scene and lifted himself up as God. He even built a shrine in defiance of God, taking the fruit of the Tree of the Knowledge of Good and Evil to a new height. Nimrod introduced a rival religion. God had to silence him with judgment, but we still feel the sting of his sin. But out of the shambles of human government sprang a light of hope. One man listened to the Word of God.

His name was Abram, but God changed his name to Abraham, meaning "father of many" or "multitude." Abraham heard the voice of God and obeyed. It is amazing what one man's obedience can do; it can even change the course of history. In an evil and idolatrous world, one man decided to obey the Word of God, and he came to be known as the Father of the Faithful. But even he could not bend the masses toward righteousness. For this reason, God tried a different approach with Abraham's children.

God's law is etched in stone. It is immutable, as eternal as God himself. No human philosophy will ever alter it. (If you are absorbed in human philosophy, you need to ALTAR it!) Unfortunately, if the Law is only written in stone, there is little hope for man, because man's nature is corrupt. The Law in stone could not turn the heart of man toward God. But the Law did introduce us to Jesus Christ and grace. "Wherefore the law was our schoolmaster to bring us unto Christ, that we might be justified by faith. But after that faith is come, we are no longer under a schoolmaster" (Galatians 3:24–25).

"Forasmuch as ye are manifestly declared to be the epistle of Christ ministered by us, written not with ink, but with the Spirit of the living God; not in tables of stone, but in fleshy tables of the heart" (II Corinthians 3:3). The law is now written in our heart. We have been born again by the Word. He has given the Holy Spirit to them that obey Him.

God has proven a point.

(1) Man sinned and destroyed his innocence.

(2) During the time of conscience, man proved that left to his own devices he will not pursue righteousness.

(3) Man proved that given the chance to govern himself he will not live righteously.

(4) Through the call of Abraham and his children, God proved that humans cannot breed righteousness.

(5) Through the Law, God showed man that righteousness cannot be legislated.

(6) It is only by grace and the regeneration by God's Spirit that righteousness can be obtained. When one is born again, he abandons his fallen carnal nature and takes on the nature of God, finding righteousness, peace, and joy in the Holy Spirit.

(7) When Jesus Christ returns to sit on His earthly throne, righteousness will reign over the earth.

What is the key to eating from the Tree of Life? Obedience to the law of God. Eden taught us that we cannot eat of both trees; we must choose one or the other. They that pursue the abstract have no right to feast on God's fruit. The wonderful truth is that they that do His commandments have the right to the Tree of Life. I will eat of the Tree of Life, for I am a concrete man in an abstract world.

∫∫

Once again Chad realized he was approaching the end of the journey. He now understood that the greatest decision one can make in life is to be obedient to God, to follow the time-proven path. He thought of the famous words of Jeremiah: "Thus saith the LORD, stand ye in the ways, and see, and ask for the old paths, where is the good way, and walk therein, and ye shall find rest for your souls."

Rest! The thought hit the young minister like a wave. "It's been a while since I really felt rested." The whole saga of his spiritual adventures hung heavily upon his heart and he found himself asking, "Was the journey really worth it? Did I make the correct decision in pursuing an advanced education? Was I wrong in opening my mind to these religious teachings?"

There was a part of him that wanted to say he would have been better off without the ideas he had encountered in seminary, that it was all a mistake, but then a strange idea came to him: "Truth is not threatened by man's knowledge."

Why should truth ever fear knowledge? Truth is a rock—a solid, absolute foundation. Truth will remain unaffected by all onslaughts of man's reasoning. It is not *knowledge* that one should fear, but *one's own spirit*. Education is not what had almost sidetracked Chad; it was his human tendency to subject God's principles to human reasoning.

He recalled some of the challenging moments in Professor Clark's class. It seemed that the eyes of the intellectual giant, for that's what he was, would drill right into Chad's soul. "Are you going to buy into the old concepts of Bible inerrancy, or are you going to reach out into the world of human potential?" What Chad saw then as an attack was most certainly a path that God had ordained for him to travel. And, though some might call it a slippery slope, it was a part of the journey that Chad would forever be grateful to have made.

Human potential! The Bible is a saga of divine intervention into human potential. The greatest potential humanity possesses seems to be the tendency to drift from God. As the psalmist said, "Every man's heart, at its best state, is altogether vanity." Is that not the story that is repeated over and over again, just changing the names of the actors? This is the slippery slope: man seeking his own path and defining his own way.

Yes, Chad was aware of the dangers. For those who believe intellect rules, this deeper learning is just the tool to reveal the true spirit within. John Foster had disappeared into the abstract, and it still grieved Chad to think of it. But was it John's quest for education that had caused his disappearance, or was it a residual, uncommitted part of his spirit that was drawn to Professor Clark's words? The Art Gallery was open to the public, so John could have made the same journey as Chad if he had so desired.

What about Dan Wilkins and Jerry Dotson? Maybe they didn't go all the way into the abstract, but they certainly fell in love with the beach house. They could have adamantly defended the faith, but when pressed with deeper issues of commitment, they preferred the feel-good message of the postmodern church.

Chad recalled a message about Moses preached by his beloved pastor. "The man of God has a twofold task. To God he represents the sinfulness of man, but to man he must represent the holiness of God." Pastor Hanson had gone on to explain that it is easy for a man to represent the failure of humanity before a holy God because, as the apostle Paul explained, all have sinned and fallen short of God's glory. However, in order for one to represent the holiness of God to mankind, the minister must climb up the mountain and remain until he can descend with the Law in his hands and the glow of anointing on his face. Dan Wilkins and Jerry Dotson had mastered the former, but they did not have the dedication and commitment to do the latter. Their philosophy seemed to be, "Let's just talk about grace and ignore the principles of holiness."

And there was Lisa Redding, the one who just wanted to be happy and get along—no debate, no conflict, no iron sharpening iron; just get along. Chad was again reminded of the famous words of Martin Luther, "Peace if possible, but truth at any rate." Lisa's destiny was wherever the river flowed. There would be no swimming against the current.

It seemed for a while that Chad was alone in his quest for absolute truth, but lately he had seen a certain look in Nicole's eyes and realized he was not alone. The journey may seem lonely at times, but the true searcher is never really alone. After all, The Art Gallery has been standing in the same place for a mighty long time.

Chad's thought processes began to slow down as he came to his conclusion. His advanced education had not been a bad choice, but a necessary part of the journey. How can one know how strong one's faith is if it is never tested? The searcher must search so that when he finds, he will know he has left no stone unturned, no idea dismissed, and no blind spots unrevealed.

Content in his spirit at last, a brand new "concrete man" turned to the last chapter of the elder's journal.

Chapter 16

Farewell

My son, I know that many have made this journey, for in my quest I have seen signs of their passing. But I have obeyed the Master Artist who commissioned me to chronicle the journey, to present a guide for any who come after me. I have spent my life searching *The Art Gallery* for myself. It is true that each person must conduct his own search, but it is beneficial to accept the word of someone who has gone before.

I now am certain I have found the truth—certain that I will remain in the land of the concrete. My days in *The Art Gallery* are over. I have obeyed His commandments and obtained my right to the Tree of Life. I will soon sink my feet in the crystal-clear water of another shore, a land much like the Garden of God, and there I will remain. But it is imperative that I leave this record behind to help others in their search.

Please go to *The Art Gallery*, to the small, private room, and look for the marble-topped cabinet. There you will find my manuscript. I hope it will encourage and strengthen you on your journey. When you come to the end, you will see me awaiting your arrival in the City of God. I will be resting beneath the Tree of Life—at last, a concrete man in a concrete world.

Chad closed the old manuscript and held it close to his heart. As he sat there, caught up in the euphoria of the moment, he sensed the presence of the Curator and turned.

"Did you find what you were searching for?" asked the Curator.

Chad gazed at him with awe and admiration, "You know I did. You knew I would find what I needed that first time I walked into your gallery."

The Curator smiled. "Yes, I believe I did."

There was a short pause in their conversation, then Chad looked at him with a hopeful yet doubtful gaze. "Sir, if I may be so bold, could I keep this manuscript? I know it is too valuable to belong to one individual, but I would like very much to keep it and treasure it."

There was a twinkle in the eye of the owner of the gallery. "Yes, you can keep it. Guard it, love it, and read it over and over again. Share it. But I must tell you there's some kind of magic in that old manuscript, for even though you have it, the next time someone like you walks into The Art Gallery, there it will be just as before, tucked away in the small, private room, hidden in the marble-topped cabinet."

Chad grasped the old parchment with both arms and stood up from the desk. He found his way back through the gallery and stepped out into the sunshine, changed, happy, and certain.

"Nicole," he thought, "I must share this with Nicole."

Epilogue

A man with graying hair sits in his recliner, surrounded by pictures of children, grandchildren, family, and friends. It seemed just yesterday that he was a troubled young man strolling down Destiny Lane searching for answers. When he discovered The Art Gallery and explored each of the rooms, he had found the answers buried in the manuscript of the elder. Thank Heaven he had found that precious parchment! Thank Heaven for the truths he had discovered at the gallery. And now, in such a short time, he himself was an elder with his own story to tell.

What a beautiful journey it had been! He remembered the day he found Nicole Freeman sitting alone at a desk in the campus library, elbows on the table, her head in her hands. Nicole was the girl who always seemed to maintain the simplicity and innocence of her faith, the girl who never wavered when others got caught up in the world of human reasoning.

Chad had paused behind her and cleared his throat.

When Nicole looked up, he saw she had been crying. She asked, "Am I the only one who believes?"

"No, you most certainly are not!" He smiled, pulled out a chair, and plopped a frayed manuscript on the table. "I have something totally awesome to share with you!"

Chad opened to the first chapter of the ancient parchment and began telling her of his experiences. Together they went through the manuscript, retracing the journey through The Art Gallery again and again. Throughout the process they fell in love with Jesus anew, they fell in love with truth anew, and somewhere on the path they fell in love with each other. Elder Chad Wittman now thought, "What an adventure it has been! While others strayed into the shady area of the abstract, Nicole and I stayed true to course, proclaiming the absolutes of the Word of God. While others reveled in their own intellect, we stuck by faith to the true wisdom James spoke about in his epistle."

Now, himself an elder, Chad sat alone in his study. It had been only a few short weeks ago that sweet Nicole had left him, and he was certain she was in a beautiful place having a personal talk with the elder author of the parchment. She had found what John Foster had once critically and erroneously proclaimed as "pie in the sky." As for Chad, it was a time for reflection—and to perform one final task.

He had been so fortunate to share his life with a beautiful woman who loved godly precepts as much as he did. Sure, hard times had come, but they remembered Jesus' proclamation that tribulation is an inevitable part of life. Through it all, there was a certain security in knowing they were doing things God's way. And God always came through.

Chad and Nicole had learned early on that trying to build God's kingdom according to human intellect limited them to their own abilities. They had trusted and waited on the sovereignty of God to open the door to the miraculous, giving them access to God's unlimited abilities. Chad recalled many exhilarating moments when the power of God would sweep into the room and miraculous changes would take place in the lives of men and women. Putting their faith in the Master Builder and aligning themselves with God's Word never stunted revival—it had always brought revival!

Like any other man reflecting back on his life, he couldn't say he was satisfied with everything he had done, but he felt a certain satisfaction about the right choices he had made. There had been a few sad days when someone they loved and invested in had slipped into the abstract never to return. These wayward souls had chosen what they called freedom, hoping for success. In reality, they found neither freedom nor success. Looking back, one thing was very clear: Obedience to the Word of God had not meant struggle and failure; rather, it had opened the door to the wonderful works of God. Chad's hands had actually touched the supernatural. What freedom there was to be found in absolute commitment to God and His Word! And success always followed doing things God's way.

The elder gazed at the walls lined with bookshelves full of commentaries, Bible dictionaries, religious books, and treatises of every kind. His eyes finally settled upon his most valued treasure—the elder's frayed parchment on display in a glass-front cabinet.

He recalled a day when Nick, his oldest son, had asked about the document. "Dad, what is that old parchment you're always reading? Is it OK if I read it?"

"Oh, son, there is no doubt you will read it someday. But you must choose a day when your mind is troubled and you're searching for something real. You probably won't open it intentionally. You'll probably . . . how can I put it . . . just stumble upon it like I did." Puzzled, the young man had simply left it at that.

☙❧

There was one final journey for Elder Wittman. He went to the display case in his study, unlocked it, and took out the parchment. Holding it securely, he made his way to The Art Gallery. Inside, it looked the same as it had when he was a young man, and interestingly enough, the Curator seemed unchanged by the years. Many memories flooded Chad's soul as the Curator escorted him to the back room where he carefully placed the manuscript in the marble-topped cabinet for the next person to find. It would help guide someone else on their journey in search of answers. He sealed it and attached a note:

Dear Curator,

I am leaving you now for the last time. Please guard my words carefully, for they are not written for entertainment. But when you see the searching look in the eyes of another young minister, please unseal this book that he may read the account of my journey. I pray his eyes will be opened to the truths I myself discovered in a parchment given to me when I visited The Art Gallery.

Sincerely, The Elder

And there it remains, awaiting your arrival.

J. STANLEY DAVIDSON

J. Stanley Davidson has served as pastor and bishop of Church on the Rock in Gadsden, Alabama, since 1984. He is the husband of Cheryl Wittman Davidson and the father of Bethany McGlaun and DeAnna Thomas. They have given him some awesome grandchildren. Stan is an ordained minister with the United Pentecostal Church International and has served the organization in numerous offices in the Alabama District, including Youth Secretary, Youth President, Presbyter, District Secretary, and District Superintendent. He has dedicated much ministry time to the training and developing of preachers and leaders. Previous published works include a Bible study series titled Sound Bible Doctrine and several music recording projects, including a number of songs that he composed.